the xo marshmallow cookbook

kat connor & lindzi shanks

Andrews McMeel
PUBLISHING®

To my wonderful husband and favorite cooking partner, Drew. You taught me to love creating in the kitchen with you by my side. I'm so lucky I get to be your sous-chef.
—Lindzi

To the ones whose anxiety brings them to the kitchen at night, who find comfort in creating, who order dessert first. This book is for you.
—Kat

To Troop XO, our fans, our friends, our recipe testers, and our biggest cheerleaders. Thank you for making the last decade filled with so much joy.

contents

3

marshmallow sidekicks & mix-ins 51

making things with marshmallows 69

5

celebrate with marshmallows 115

introduction

"wait, you can *make* marshmallows?!"

It all started at Christmas. Well, *almost* Christmas. The clock was ticking as Kat balanced law school finals, work, and the holidays. She was scrambling for a last-minute gift for her family within her limited budget and even more limited time. A brief internet search yielded the perfect treat: a mug filled with hot cocoa mix, marshmallows, and a candy cane. At the bottom of the recipe, the author of the blog post said, "To make this gift even more personal, try making your own marshmallows." She thought, *Great! How hard could that be?!* ... Y'all, it was harder than it looked. (Psst ... Don't worry—our recipes are MUCH easier!)

That original homemade marshmallow recipe was incredibly complicated. The ingredients list included: vanilla beans roasted by hand, a variety of invert sugars, organic egg whites, and tapioca starch to coat them. After quite a bit of prep work, the process became more straightforward. The yield of that batch was enough to top a few dozen mug sets, which Kat gave out to her coworkers, classmates, friends, and family.

The feedback was all the same: "Wait, you MADE these marshmallows?!" Kat shrugged it off and got back to studying. But more and more frequently, people brought up that first batch and asked for more. No one had ever tried anything like this before.

After graduating, Kat moved back home to Chicago and decided to take a small break before jumping into the law-related job market. She ended up working at a local cafe, where she was able to use the back kitchen to experiment with marshmallow recipes and flavors and test some ideas out on customers. In June, Kat launched the "XO Marshmallow" brand with a batch of rainbow marshmallows inspired by the LGBTQ+ Pride Parade. Over the next few months, she kept concepting marshmallow flavor combinations and learned everything she could to make them better.

Almost a year after that first batch of mallows, Kat was again up against the clock for the holidays. She had run through a lot of her personal savings and needed some extra cash to make it through Christmas. She saw an Instagram post asking for seasonal help at a pop-up shop downtown and applied.

pop the bubbly . . . or don't

On the other side of Chicago lived Lindzi, who had similarly taken a sidestep from pursuing an industry job in psychology after obtaining her master's and was running a clothing and accessories boutique instead. Lindzi had seen the potential of the Etsy marketplace when the platform first launched and had also gained a strong following on social media. It was good sense with good timing that got her a physical storefront, and thanks to a bit of kismet, she and Kat met during Kat's interview. At that point, Kat mentioned making marshmallows, and Lindzi offered to sell them in the shop.

At the close of the pop-up, the marshmallows with Lindzi's graphic mugs were the bestselling item. Lindzi said she saw the potential of XO in e-commerce and as a brand with a big impact on social media.

"Would you be interested in becoming business partners?" Lindzi asked.

"No," Kat said. They barely knew each other and, sure, a successful partnership sounded great (in theory), but what would happen if the business flopped and Kat went back to job hunting?

Luckily, the story doesn't end there. After some convincing, a few more chats, and a few shared laughs, they decided to give this XO Marshmallow idea a real shot. In January 2016, they agreed to each put $100 into a joint bank account. The XO Marshmallow brand was born. They had no idea how life-changing that decision would be.

Their first order of business was figuring out packaging. They knew they wanted something giftable that sat well on a shelf and that would hold about a dozen marshmallows. They also wanted something that was unique, fun, and whimsical and that spoke to marshmallow lovers of all ages. They tested and settled on a few core flavors, including Salted Caramel, Lavender Honey, Champagne, and Coffee Kahlúa. Kat figured they would have a website up and running in the first few months of becoming partners, but Lindzi had it up within a week. XO was live on Etsy with a handful of orders, but they were still buying ingredients at the local grocery store and working off the same vintage 5-quart mixer.

the first marshmallow cafe

In the first year of business, Kat and Lindzi sold marshmallows at every market they could bargain their way into and worked diligently on getting their e-commerce orders up. But customers were constantly asking where people could shop XO *in person*. In early 2017, they decided to host a Kickstarter campaign, figuring that if their customer base really wanted a retail location filled with marshmallowy goodness, they could help support it. It turned out that people were just as excited about marshmallows as Kat and Lindzi were, as this Kickstarter was successfully funded; they began working on the world's first marshmallow cafe.

The XO Marshmallow Cafe opened on July 1, 2017. That morning, Lindzi and Kat hid behind the counter, trying to catch their breath.

"What if no one shows up?"

"What if everyone hates the menu?"

"OMG, what are we doing?! Should we just sneak out the back?"

"What if no one loves marshmallows as much as we do?"

"This was the worst idea."

After about ten minutes of nail-biting panic, they decided they would unlock the door. And if no one came in, they could just . . . run away. Or something.

They peeked over the counter, and their stomachs dropped. In the small 500-foot space that made up the cafe was a window that looked out to the sidewalk. And no one was there. They were about ten minutes past opening time and, with clenched hands, they nervously made their way up the few hand-built steps to unlock the door. Time to run.

At that point, Kat heard the click of the lock but wasn't sure which of them had turned it. The two pulled the heavy metal handle back and stepped into the sunlight. A line of families, friends, Kickstarter supporters, and strangers were camped down the block, around the corner, and were spilling into the street. They had left a small clearing near the front window so as not to block the door, making them invisible from Kat and Lindzi's hiding spot. They had all shown up.

So many s'mores were shared that day. And from that summer on, they were able to expand their team and menu. They began making their own gluten-free graham crackers and other marshmallow-inspired treats. The cafe brought more attention to their now-booming website, and the website reminded folks to visit them if they were coming to Chicago. They went viral often and appeared on television shows like *Today* and *The Chew* and in publications such as *Buzzfeed*, *Food & Wine*, *Refinery29*, and more.

Over the next few years, they continued to grow and learned more about business management, food packaging, and evolving their message to bring the joy of marshmallows to the world.

a new lease on xo life

In 2022, Kat and Lindzi moved their cafe and production space, creating a new home for both. The XO Headquarters (XO HQ for short) moved to a large warehouse with rainbow floors and a dock—a true Willy Wonka dream come true! The new cafe opened in June 2022 in Lincoln Park with almost triple the square footage of the original space and beautiful, colorful murals. On opening day, they did *not* hide behind the counter but greeted waiting customers like old friends, some of whom were at their first grand opening a few years prior.

It was a year of great transition. They dealt with moves, supply chain issues, learning management styles, personal tragedies, and triumphs. They were a natural pairing. Kat had all the kitchen skills. Lindzi had none (though she has since developed her culinary skills). Lindzi lived for social media marketing and creating the perfect brand. Kat recoiled from Instagram (although she has also come around). That dynamic resulted in a lot of the success for XO Marshmallow—with Kat constantly working to make everything taste delicious, and Lindzi creating a colorful brand that people wanted to be part of.

You'll see this theme throughout this book: the balance of taste and, well, *taste*!

the science and magic of marshmallow making

Kat and Lindzi, the cofounders of XO Marshmallow, share the secrets of their s'more success! Making marshmallows is part science, part magic—this book contains more than eighty delicious marshmallow-centric recipes, ranging from classic Salted-Caramel Marshmallows (page 33) to putting together the perfect marshmallow charcuterie board (page 117). This cookbook is all about adding the ingredient your kitchen (and dare we say, life) has been missing—the beloved marshmallow—and turning it into something far greater: a delicious dessert in its own right.

1

marshmallow-making essentials

Candy making has a rich history—added to by chefs, scientists, and even really inventive home chefs, like you! This chapter explores the delicious history and technical components of marshmallow making, along with the equipment and ingredients needed to set yourself up for delectable success.

a bit about marshmallows (according to kat and lindzi)

Marshmallows are an aerated confection made with sugar, gelatin, and glucose syrup. They are springy and light and can be flavored in a variety of ways. Marshmallows got their name from the marsh mallow plant, *Althaea officinalis,* an herb with a sticky sap and white floral leaves. The marsh mallow plant was often used to heal wounds and soothe sore throats, with evidence of its use dating back to the ancient Egyptians and again in medieval Europe.

In the late nineteenth century, in France, confectioners began experimenting with marsh mallow sap and found that whipping it with egg whites and sugar produced a delicious, soft candy. Eventually, the plant sap was replaced with gelatin, adding much-needed stabilization.

In the twentieth century, industrialization provided more opportunities to automate the process of candy making, and the access to sugar and gelatin made making marshmallows especially appealing. The sweet treats went from being sold in small tins to being mass produced and extruded into new shapes and sizes. By the 1950s, marshmallows had developed a reputation for being a staple in every household and were often featured in desserts ranging from rice crispy cereal treats to s'mores. Speaking of s'mores—did you know that s'mores were a treat invented by the Girl Scouts in 1927? #girlpower

In the 1990s, we grew up snacking and baking with store-bought marshmallows, and it wasn't until 2014, when Kat whipped up her first batch of homemade marshmallows, that we realized *gourmet* marshmallows were a possibility. No longer were we confined to the large boring plastic bag so many Americans had become accustomed to. Since then, XO Marshmallow has produced over one hundred flavored marshmallows and treats for the world to enjoy. And now? We are excited to bring you a cookbook so you can make these treats at home for you and your loved ones.

the science of making marshmallows

We always say that making marshmallows is "part science and part magic." The science comes in the form of sugar syrup being heated to a particular temperature and whipped together with a protein. As the mixture cools and air is introduced, the sugar molecules re-form and bind with the proteins to create the final product—a marshmallow. Most candies use a heated sugar syrup, and marshmallows fall in the lower temperature of the candy-making spectrum—around 240°F.

In our process, we combine sugar, water, and corn syrup for our sugar syrup mix. The corn syrup acts as our invert sugar, which is really just a fancy way of saying that it breaks down the granulated sugar into glucose and fructose, allowing it to start the chemical process of candy making. We then use gelatin as the protein and often add extracts or color to enhance the final marshmallow. Gelatin is a thermoreversible protein, meaning it can heat, cool, and re-form—you can see this magic happen when you toast a marshmallow over a campfire. Notice how it gets brown and toasty and a little melted? Perfection.

Similar to the process of making marshmallows is making marshmallow cream or, as we like to call it, Ooey Marshmallow Goodness (OMG) (page 48). Instead of gelatin, we use egg whites to stabilize our mixture, and the result is a creamy, spreadable marshmallow.

When it comes to adding flavors, one thing to note is the amount of liquid you are introducing to the base recipe and the amount of fat. Some mix-ins can deflate your marshmallow if added too quickly (like Salted-Caramel Sauce, page 54), and some mix-ins taste best when infused in the water called for at the beginning of the recipe (like lavender).

The magic kicks in after your first few batches. There will be slip-ups, flip-flops, and very sticky messes to clean up. But after awhile, you will begin to *sense* when a batch is ready. You will *feel* the perfect moment to add in that extract, and you will achieve the level of marshmallow wizardry that our team does every day. It's a great feeling!

essential equipment

There are some things that make using this book a bit easier. Below are a few ingredients and tools we recommend for making the best confections. Of course, we are big believers in using what you have on hand, so where applicable, we will recommend a suitable substitute.

STAND MIXER: Marshmallows are an aerated confection, and aerating them by hand is very difficult. We recommend a sturdy stand mixer to do the whisking for you. In some recipes, a hand mixer will work just fine. For our marshmallow and OMG recipe, we recommend a 5-quart or 6-quart mixer. If you plan on making a mess of marshmallows, an extra bowl and whisk will come in handy.

CANDY THERMOMETER: Aside from a mixer, this is probably the most essential item for making candy. Candy thermometers can read temperatures as low as 100°F and as high as 400°F. They can either be analog or digital, and most have a clip that allows them to safely attach to the side of a pan. You can typically find candy thermometers at any baking supply store, specialty food/craft stores, or online.

HEAVY-BOTTOM POTS: You will need at least one 6-quart heavy-bottom pot to make the sugar syrup for the marshmallows. We often call for these pots in our recipes because they can withstand high temperatures, and the sides are tall enough to keep you from getting splashes of hot sugar all over you. Win-win! We recommend having a few pots on hand because some recipes need more room than others.

8 BY 8-INCH OR 9 BY 9-INCH PANS: Our marshmallow recipes are best prepared using 8 by 8-inch or 9 by 9-inch pans. You can easily double the recipe for 9 by 13-inch pans.

MEASURING CUPS AND SPOONS: Liquid and dry measuring cups are essential for accurate measuring while baking. Measuring spoons are also

used when measuring out smaller ingredients like extracts, salt, and other spices. For more accurate measuring, we recommend investing in a small kitchen scale.

SET OF WHISKS, SPOONS, AND SPATULAS: Each recipe will list the best utensils, but having a set of whisks, wooden spoons, and spatulas on hand can make the process run a bit smoother. A high-heat-resistant spatula is especially useful when making candy.

CUTTING BOARD AND KNIFE: Flipping a batch of marshmallows out of the pan and cutting them up might be the best part of the marshmallow-making process—it's certainly our fans' favorite thing to watch on social media. A knife works just fine and can be wiped down and sprayed with unflavored nonstick pan spray as needed. Additionally, you can use what we call a "bench scraper" to cut your marshmallows. These are hard-sided metal tools with a wood or plastic handle and are easy for kids (and Lindzi) to handle.

AIRTIGHT CONTAINERS: You'll want to store your marshmallows in an airtight container at room temperature. We tend to have a few containers at the ready for all of our treats, frostings, and other open ingredients.

essential ingredients

Each recipe will list all the ingredients needed to make the most delicious treat. However, there are a few that pop up again and again, so it is worth getting larger quantities of the following:

SUGAR: Most recipes will use granulated white sugar.

GELATIN: Marshmallow recipes utilize gelatin as the protein that binds together sugar molecules and creates that spongy, soft confection. Gelatin is a protein made from animal collagen. Most commercially available gelatins are made using pork or beef. All these recipes were tested using kosher beef gelatin. You can find gelatin at most grocery stores in the baking aisle, but some online retailers may offer more variety.

CORN SYRUP: This is a glucose syrup used to prevent crystallization during the marshmallow-making process. All of our recipes were tested with Karo corn syrup but can be substituted with any other corn syrup or glucose syrup. Corn syrup can be replaced with equal parts honey (Honey Marshmallows, page 30) or can be cut with agave to reduce the amount of syrup present.

CONFECTIONERS' SUGAR AND CORNSTARCH: We combine these ingredients to make the coating for our marshmallows. The coating powder helps prevent them from sticking together. You can easily substitute part or all of the sugar and starch with other starches such as potato or tapioca. Just be mindful that it may affect the taste of your finished product.

GREASING THE PAN: Nothing is worse than trying to flip a perfect batch of marshmallows out of the pan only to find that they are stuck—we know. We've done it A LOT. When it comes to greasing the pan, we recommend unflavored nonstick pan spray. Using other sprays that contain coconut, butter, or artificial flavoring may leave a lingering flavor on the marshmallows.

ADDING FLAVOR: You can add fresh fruit, extracts, sprinkles, and more to your marshmallows! Be mindful that what you add may have more water content, so other elements may need to be adjusted. For example, if you want to make a spiced apple cider marshmallow, you can replace the water in the recipe for fresh apple cider—but since apples and apple cider tend to have added sugar, reduce the amount of sugar called for in the recipe by 2 tablespoons. You can also reduce the apple cider down to a concentrate for a more potent flavor. We recommend finding the best extracts and mix-ins in your budget.

ADDING COLOR: Some ingredients will add a natural color to the final treat. However, you can add food coloring to almost any recipe. We recommend liquid food coloring or gel food coloring. More and more natural food coloring is becoming available (yay!), but some additions may impact the flavor of your finished marshmallows.

dos and don'ts of making marshmallows

Remember when we said that marshmallow making was part science and part magic? Well, candy making is very scientific, but we know there are moments when everything can go very wrong or come together in an instant. Here are some tips and tricks to getting it right:

First, don't take your eyes off the process. Sugar can burn the moment you walk away. Butter will go from brown to stuck-to-the-bottom-of-the-pot in a matter of seconds. Pay attention, and not only will you begin to master the art of marshmallow making but you will also save time by catching mistakes. First, find a candy thermometer that has an automatic alarm to let you know when you are close to the desired temperature.

Second, prep out everything. In the culinary world, this is called "mise en place," which means "everything in its place." Most professional chefs weigh and measure out every ingredient before ever touching a recipe, and we recommend doing that too. This practice will ensure you have everything you need because nothing is worse than being two-thirds of the way through a recipe before realizing you don't have enough sugar! In candy making, things happen *fast*, so it's best to have your ingredients and your tools at the ready.

Third, find the best ingredients you can afford. These recipes were tested with ingredients commonly found in grocery stores, but almost everything will be enhanced by sourcing fresh, artisanal, and local ingredients. A higher percentage of chocolate means a higher percentage of cocoa bean and, therefore, a darker, richer chocolate cake. Puree farmer's market berries for a sweet and fresh mallow. Natural food color can add a tint to your dessert and keep it allergen free. There are lots of options to experiment with, and we encourage you to try them all!

Finally, there are a few ways a batch of marshmallows may not turn out. Maybe they are under- or over-whipped. Maybe the candy thermometer needs to be recalibrated. Maybe the bowl had water in it, so the egg whites didn't floof up correctly. We are here to help, so reach out to us with your marshmallow-making questions. Most importantly, don't get discouraged. We've made ALL the mistakes and have learned from them. Sometimes the best thing to do is stop, reset, and try again. You've got this. Now, let's make some marshmallows!

2

marshmallow recipes

Making candy can be intimidating. Most people are worried about handling hot sugar syrup or swirling a pan filled with caramel sauce. Fear not, young confectioners! These recipes are written to (safely) take you step-by-step through the process of making marshmallows. Once you've mastered the fundamentals, you'll be empowered to experiment and truly make them your own.

vanilla marshmallows

MAKES 36 MARSHMALLOWS

Homemade marshmallows are both the simplest and the most humbling of confectionary treats. Back in 2014, in my tiny kitchen with my tiny (twenty-year-old) mixer, I undertook one of the most complicated recipes I have ever encountered. I spent an hour roasting and seeding a vanilla bean pod. And while I always love fresh vanilla, I found that in my many marshmallow batches since, there are ways to simplify a recipe. So that's what I did—I experimented with sugars, temperatures, adding flavors, and clarifying some of the more technical language in candy making. I will forever be grateful for that first recipe; it sparked an adventure that has changed my life. I hope that you find this process simple to follow and that you will share, re-create, and enjoy for celebrations big and small. —KAT

Unflavored nonstick pan spray

1 cup cold water, divided

3 tablespoons gelatin

1 cup corn syrup

1½ cups granulated sugar

½ teaspoon kosher salt

1 tablespoon vanilla extract

Cornstarch or tapioca starch, for dusting

Confectioners' sugar, for dusting

Prep an 8 by 8-inch or 9 by 9-inch pan with a thin layer of unflavored nonstick pan spray. Set aside.

In a small microwave-safe bowl, pour ½ cup cold water and sprinkle the gelatin on top. Use a small whisk to combine and set aside. This process is called *blooming the gelatin*.

In a heavy-bottom 6 or 8-quart pan, combine the corn syrup, sugar, remaining ½ cup water, and salt. Cook over medium heat, occasionally swirling the pan until the sugar dissolves. After this point, do not stir or swirl the syrup in the pan.

Clip a candy thermometer into the pan and raise the temperature to high heat until the syrup reaches 240°F. This is known as the *soft ball stage* in candy making.

Once the syrup in the pan reaches 240°F, remove from heat and allow to cool to 220°F, then carefully pour into the bowl of the stand mixer.

Heat the gelatin in the microwave on 50 percent power for 30-second intervals until liquid, between 1 and 2 minutes total. Then pour the gelatin mixture into the bowl of your stand mixer fitted with the whisk attachment.

Turn the mixer on low and allow the syrup to combine with the gelatin. This is a good time to run your saucepan to the sink and soak with warm, soapy water.

Increase the mixer speed to medium for 3 to 5 minutes, allowing the mixture to become frothy and lighten in color. Then increase the speed to high for about 10 minutes until the mixture is thick and glossy. Add the vanilla extract. You will know the marshmallow is ready when it has tripled in volume and starts to "pull" away from the edges of the bowl.

Working quickly, use a spatula to scoop the marshmallow from the bowl into the prepared pan. Spread out into an even layer. Let rest for at least 4 hours, uncovered, at room temperature.

Meanwhile, in a small bowl, mix one part cornstarch with three parts confectioners' sugar for dusting. This is called *coating powder*.

When the marshmallows are set, they will be slightly tacky and matte in color. Using a fine sieve, sprinkle some of the dusting mixture over the top of the marshmallow. Then run a sharp knife around the edge of your pan to loosen the marshmallow.

Flip the pan over onto a cutting board and dust the exposed marshmallow with more coating powder.

Cut into squares, then toss with a bit more coating powder. Enjoy! Marshmallows are best stored in a cool, dry place. Store in an airtight container for 2 weeks and enjoy as a snack, in your hot cocoa, or toasted in an ooey, gooey s'more.

TIP: Marshmallows will continue to dry when exposed to air. For the perfect s'more, leave the freshly coated and cut marshmallows out for about an hour. This will allow them to better hold their shape and not melt *too* quickly when toasted.

vanilla MarsHalos™

MAKES 24 LARGE OR 48 SMALL MARSHALOS™

One night, late in the kitchen, I ended up with an extra floofy batch of marshmallows. I happened to have a donut pan nearby and quickly scooped the marshmallow goo into the cavities. Before you could even say "hot cocoa!" we launched our MarsHalos™—donut-shaped marshmallows made perfectly for mugs. These 'Halos ended up becoming a feature in our first Kickstarter campaign in 2016 and garnered our first real bit of publicity. They won an award, which allowed us free advertising in the *Chicago Tribune,* which led to more sleepless nights in the kitchen and created a lot of demand for our cafe space.

The best part about this recipe is that you can make MarsHalos™ out of any of our marshmallow recipes! Create your own and set up a hot cocoa bar (page 139) for the holidays. —**KAT**

Follow the steps for Vanilla Marshmallows (page 18). However, instead of preparing a pan, prepare donut pans. You can use larger pans, with six cavities, or smaller pans, with a dozen cavities.

Add the marshmallow mixture to piping bags and, working quickly, fill each cavity with the marshmallow mixture. Let rest for at least 3 hours or until the marshmallows are tacky to the touch.

Sprinkle the tops with the coating power. Using a sharp knife, gently extract each MarsHalo™ from the pan and move onto a coated surface. Cover with more coating powder.

NOTE: MarsHalos™ can be flavored with extracts or colored with food coloring. You can even mix cocoa powder with coating powder for a touch of chocolate!

lavender-honey marshmallows

Lindzi loves lavender. Actually, so does my mom. When we were first concepting our core marshmallow flavors, lavender was immediately a front-runner. I was hesitant about the floral flavor coming off as too "soapy," but after a few . . . subtle . . . hints from fans (*cough* Lindzi *cough*), we decided to give it a go. What I love about this recipe is that the honey balances the marshmallow flavor, giving it depth. Also, as honey is a natural invert sugar, it plays a pivotal role in the candy-making process and is an easy substitute for corn syrup if you are looking for one. The first test batch of lavender–honey marshmallows disappeared quickly, which was a sure sign that we had a hit. While Lindzi can snack on an entire box, I prefer to enjoy one or two marshmallows with some tea (recipe follows). —KAT

1 cup cold water

1 tablespoon culinary-grade lavender buds

Unflavored nonstick pan spray

3 tablespoons gelatin

½ cup corn syrup

½ cup honey

1½ cups granulated sugar

½ teaspoon kosher salt

1 tablespoon vanilla extract

Purple food coloring (optional)

Cornstarch or tapioca starch, for dusting

Confectioners' sugar, for dusting

Add the water to the base of a small saucepan. Add the lavender buds and bring to a boil over medium-high heat. Remove the saucepan from the heat and allow the water and lavender buds to steep for 10 minutes. Then strain the water using a sieve and remove all the lavender pieces. Chill the water in the refrigerator until cold. The infused water may be made ahead of time and will keep in the fridge for up to 3 days.

Prepare an 8 by 8-inch or 9 by 9-inch pan with a thin layer of unflavored nonstick pan spray. Set aside.

In a small microwave-safe bowl, pour ½ cup cold lavender water and sprinkle the gelatin on top. Use a small whisk to combine and set aside. This process is called *blooming* the gelatin.

In a heavy-bottom 6 or 8-quart pan, combine the corn syrup, honey, sugar, remaining ½ cup lavender water, and salt. Cook over medium heat, occasionally swirling the pan until the sugar dissolves. After this point, do not stir or swirl the syrup in the pan.

continued

Clip a candy thermometer to the pan and raise the temperature to high heat until the syrup reaches 240°F. This is known as the *soft ball stage* in candy making.

Once the syrup in the pan reaches 240°F, remove from heat and allow to cool to 220°F, then carefully pour into the bowl of the stand mixer.

Heat the gelatin in the microwave on 50 percent power for 30-second intervals until liquid, between 1 and 2 minutes total. Then pour the gelatin mixture into the bowl of your stand mixer fitted with the whisk attachment. This is a good time to run your saucepan to the sink and soak with warm, soapy water.

Increase the mixer speed to medium for 3 to 5 minutes, allowing the mixture to become frothy and lighten in color. Then increase the speed to high for about 10 minutes until the mixture is thick and glossy. Add the vanilla extract and food coloring, if using. You will know the marshmallow is ready when it has tripled in volume and starts to "pull" away from the edges of the bowl.

Working quickly, use a spatula to scoop the marshmallow from the bowl into the prepared pan. Spread out into an even layer. Let rest for at least 4 hours, uncovered, at room temperature.

Meanwhile, in a small bowl, mix one part cornstarch with three parts confectioners' sugar for dusting. This is called *coating powder*.

When the marshmallows are set, they will be slightly tacky and matte in color. Using a fine sieve, sprinkle some of the dusting mixture over the top of the marshmallow. Then run a sharp knife around the edge of your pan to loosen the marshmallow. Flip the pan over onto a cutting board and dust the exposed marshmallow with more coating powder.

Cut into squares, then toss with a bit more coating powder. Enjoy! Marshmallows are best stored in a cool, dry place. Store in an airtight container for 2 weeks and enjoy as a snack, in your hot cocoa, or toasted in an ooey, gooey s'more.

TIP: Marshmallows will continue to dry when exposed to air. For the perfect s'more, leave freshly coated and cut marshmallows out for about an hour. This will allow them to better hold their shape and not melt *too* quickly when toasted.

NOTES: Honey is used here as an invert sugar and performs an important function in the marshmallow-making process. There are many varieties of honey available, and the underlying notes will come forward as the marshmallow sets. Pure honey will have a deeper, more powerful, honey-forward taste, whereas wildflower honey will complement the lavender base. Pay attention to the variety of honey you use, but have fun!

Make sure to purchase culinary-grade lavender buds, also known as English lavender. Culinary lavender is food safe and ideal for use in baking and cooking because it contains less oil than its more aromatic cousin. Double-check your lavender to prevent a "soapy" flavor and preserve the right amount of floral.

xo's lavender london fog

A traditional London fog is Earl Grey tea steeped in cream or milk with vanilla. These Lavender–Honey marshmallows add a creamy, sweet flavor, and the aromatics of the lavender buds really come through in a subtle and soothing way.

In your favorite mug, steep Earl Grey tea for 2 to 5 minutes in 8 ounces of boiling water.

Top with two Lavender-Honey marshmallows and allow to melt completely, stirring to cool. Take a deep breath over the mug to enjoy the aroma of soothing lavender and citrus bergamot. Enjoy.

coffee marshmallows

Coffee marshmallows were the first flavor that made me stop and say, *Wow, this could really be something special!* And, yes, I am a bit biased. In college and law school, you could find me with a book in one hand and a coffee in the other. I love coffee-flavored everything, including a recipe for coffee frosting from the early '90s in which you swap out the liquid for brewed coffee. Simple, right? Cut to 2015, my law school graduation party, and a sweet s'mores bar filled with my first-ever flavored homemade marshmallows. Coffee marshmallows, made by swapping out the water for brewed coffee, became the star of the evening. Friends and family members kept cornering me, telling me they had never had anything like them and encouraging me to keep experimenting with gourmet marshmallow flavors. We have done so much with coffee since then, from adding Kahlúa for a boozy twist, to collaborating with some pretty amazing coffee brands, to developing our caffeinated marshmallows for that extra buzz. Enjoy these mallows on their own or toasted on top of a latte. —KAT

Unflavored nonstick pan spray

1 cup chilled strongly brewed coffee, divided

3 tablespoons gelatin

1 cup corn syrup

1½ cups granulated sugar

½ teaspoon kosher salt

1 tablespoon vanilla extract

Cornstarch or tapioca starch, for dusting

Confectioners' sugar, for dusting

Prepare an 8 by 8-inch or 9 by 9-inch pan with a thin layer of unflavored nonstick pan spray. Set aside.

In a small microwave-safe bowl, pour ½ cup chilled coffee and sprinkle the gelatin on top. Use a small whisk to combine and set aside. This process is called *blooming* the gelatin.

In a heavy-bottom 6 or 8-quart pan, combine the corn syrup, sugar, remaining ½ cup coffee, and salt. Cook over medium heat, occasionally swirling the pan until the sugar dissolves. After this point, do not stir or swirl the syrup in the pan.

Clip a candy thermometer to the pan and raise the temperature to high heat until the syrup reaches 240°F. This is known as the *soft ball stage* in candy making.

continued

Once the syrup in the pan reaches 240°F, remove from heat and allow to cool to 220°F, then carefully pour into the bowl of the stand mixer.

Heat the gelatin in the microwave on 50 percent power for 30-second intervals until liquid, between 1 and 2 minutes total. Then pour the gelatin mixture into the bowl of your stand mixer fitted with the whisk attachment. This is a good time to run your saucepan to the sink and soak with warm, soapy water.

Increase the mixer speed to medium for 3 to 5 minutes, allowing the mixture to become frothy and lighten in color. Then increase the speed to high for about 10 minutes until the mixture is thick and glossy. Add the vanilla extract. You will know the marshmallow is ready when it has tripled in volume and starts to "pull" away from the edges of the bowl.

Working quickly, use a spatula to scoop the marshmallow from the bowl into the prepared pan. Spread out into an even layer. Let rest for at least 4 hours, uncovered, at room temperature.

Meanwhile, in a small bowl, mix one part cornstarch with three parts confectioners' sugar for dusting. This is called *coating powder*.

When the marshmallows are set, they will be slightly tacky and matte in color. Using a fine sieve, sprinkle some of the dusting mixture over the top of the marshmallow.

Then run a sharp knife around the edge of your pan to loosen the marshmallow. Flip the pan over onto a cutting board and dust the exposed marshmallow with more coating powder.

Cut into squares, then toss with a bit more coating powder. Enjoy! Marshmallows are best stored in a cool, dry place. Store in an airtight container for 2 weeks and enjoy as a snack, in your hot cocoa, or toasted in an ooey, gooey s'more.

TIP: Marshmallows will continue to dry when exposed to air. For the perfect s'more, leave the freshly coated and cut marshmallows out for about an hour. This will allow them to better hold their shape and not melt *too* quickly when toasted.

NOTES: To reduce the amount of caffeine, simply swap in an equal amount of decaf coffee, or follow the Vanilla Marshmallows recipe (page 18) and use coffee extract instead of vanilla extract in the final stage.

Instant coffee can be used instead of brewed coffee. Simply heat 1 cup of water, add 1 tablespoon of instant coffee, and stir to combine. Chill ½ cup to use in the gelatin mixture, and use the remaining ½ cup in the pot.

mocha marshmallows

Add 1 tablespoon dark cocoa powder to the coating; mix until thoroughly combined. Follow steps to coat with cocoa coating for a chocolate-espresso variation.

kahlúa marshmallows

Add 2 tablespoons Kahlúa liqueur to the saucepan during the syrup stage for a boozy mallow.

honey marshmallows
(corn syrup free)

If you are trying to limit the amount of sugar in your marshmallows, try this easy swap. Honey is a natural sweetener and can be used as a one-to-one substitute for corn syrup. Just note that you will want a bigger heavy-bottom saucepan for this recipe because hot honey loves to escape. We used pure honey in this recipe, but you can experiment with flavored honey as well.
—LINDZI

Unflavored nonstick pan spray

1 cup cold water, divided

3 tablespoons gelatin

1 cup pure honey

1½ cups granulated sugar

½ teaspoon kosher salt

1 tablespoon vanilla extract

Cornstarch or tapioca starch, for dusting

Confectioners' sugar, for dusting

Prepare an 8 by 8-inch or 9 by 9-inch pan with a thin layer of unflavored nonstick pan spray. Set aside.

In a small microwave-safe bowl, pour ½ cup cold water and sprinkle the gelatin on top. Use a small whisk to combine and set aside. This process is called *blooming* the gelatin.

In a heavy-bottom 10 or 12-quart pan, combine the pure honey, sugar, remaining ½ cup water, and salt. Cook over medium heat, occasionally swirling the pan until the sugar dissolves. After this point, do not stir or swirl the syrup in the pan. If the syrup starts to climb up the sides of the pan and you are worried it may spill over, simply lower the heat. This process takes a bit longer than traditional marshmallows, but it's worth it!

Clip a candy thermometer to the pan and raise the temperature to high heat until the syrup reaches 240°F. This is known as the *soft ball stage* in candy making.

Once the syrup in the pan reaches 240°F, remove from heat and allow to cool to 220°F, then carefully pour into the bowl of the stand mixer.

continued

Heat the gelatin in the microwave on 50 percent power for 30-second intervals until liquid, between 1 and 2 minutes total. Then pour the gelatin mixture into the bowl of your stand mixer fitted with the whisk attachment. This is a good time to run your saucepan to the sink and soak with warm, soapy water.

Increase the mixer speed to medium for 3 to 5 minutes, allowing the mixture to become frothy and lighten in color. Then increase the speed to high for about 10 minutes until the mixture is thick and glossy. Add the vanilla extract. You will know the marshmallow is ready when it has tripled in volume and starts to "pull" away from the edges of the bowl.

Working quickly, use a spatula to scoop the marshmallow from the bowl into the prepared pan. Spread out into an even layer. Let rest for at least 4 hours, uncovered, at room temperature.

Meanwhile, in a small bowl, mix one part cornstarch with three parts confectioners' sugar for dusting. This is called *coating powder*.

When the marshmallows are set, they will be slightly tacky and matte in color. Using a fine sieve, sprinkle some of the dusting mixture over the top of the marshmallow. Then run a sharp knife around the edge of your pan to loosen the marshmallow. Flip the pan over onto a cutting board and dust the exposed marshmallow with more coating powder.

Cut into squares, then toss with a bit more coating powder. Enjoy! Marshmallows are best stored in a cool, dry place. Store in an airtight container for 2 weeks and enjoy as a snack, in your hot cocoa, or toasted in an ooey, gooey s'more.

TIP: Marshmallows will continue to dry when exposed to air. For the perfect s'more, leave the freshly coated and cut marshmallows out for about an hour. This will allow them to better hold their shape and not melt *too* quickly when toasted.

salted-caramel marshmallows

From an early age, I knew I loved caramel. While we never made it at home, we would often find soft caramels when we were out shopping or had a handful of hard caramel candies sitting in a candy dish somewhere. I loved the sweet and toasted warmth that only caramel flavor could provide—it just went with everything.

As an adult, I find that salted caramel has become an elevated flavor particularly popular in America. But did you know that salted caramel originated in France, when chocolatier Henri Le Roux created a recipe using salted butter to differentiate himself from his competition? His *caramel au beurre salé* started a craze for all things salted caramel in the late 1970s and now is considered a contemporary classic for all things sweet.

When experimenting with flavors back in 2016, we found that the salt in the salted-caramel recipe both balanced and enhanced the sweetness of the marshmallow. We love this flavor because it is equal parts nostalgic and elegant—fun and fancy—and since its first release, this marshmallow has been a customer favorite. Bon appétit! **—KAT**

Unflavored nonstick pan spray

1 cup cold water, divided

3 tablespoons gelatin

1 cup corn syrup

1½ cups granulated sugar

½ teaspoon kosher salt

1 tablespoon vanilla extract

½ cup Salted-Caramel Sauce (page 54)

Cornstarch or tapioca starch, for dusting

Confectioners' sugar, for dusting

Prepare an 8 by 8-inch or 9 by 9-inch pan with a thin layer of unflavored nonstick pan spray. Set aside.

In a small microwave-safe bowl, pour ½ cup cold water and sprinkle the gelatin on top. Use a small whisk to combine and set aside. This process is called *blooming* the gelatin.

In a heavy-bottom 6 or 8-quart pan, combine the corn syrup, sugar, remaining ½ cup water, and salt. Cook over medium heat, occasionally swirling the pan until the sugar dissolves. After this point, do not stir or swirl the syrup in the pan.

continued

Clip a candy thermometer to the pan and raise the temperature to high heat until the syrup reaches 240°F. This is known as the *soft ball stage* in candy making.

Once the syrup in the pan reaches 240°F, remove from heat and allow to cool to 220°F, then carefully pour into the bowl of the stand mixer.

Heat the gelatin in the microwave on 50 percent power for 30-second intervals until liquid, between 1 and 2 minutes total. Then pour the gelatin mixture into the bowl of your stand mixer fitted with the whisk attachment. This is a good time to run your saucepan to the sink and soak with warm, soapy water.

Increase the mixer speed to medium for 3 to 5 minutes, allowing the mixture to become frothy and lighten in color. Then increase the speed to high for about 10 minutes until the mixture is thick and glossy. Add the vanilla extract. You will know the marshmallow is ready when it has tripled in volume and starts to "pull" away from the edges of the bowl.

Working quickly, use a spatula to swirl in the Salted-Caramel Sauce (page 54) in large figure eight motions. Do no more than four figure eight motions or the marshmallow will start to deflate. Then pour the marshmallow from the bowl into the prepared pan. Spread out into an even layer. Let rest for at least 4 hours, uncovered, at room temperature. Meanwhile, in a small bowl, mix one part cornstarch with three parts confectioners' sugar for dusting. This is called *coating powder*.

When the marshmallows are set, they will be slightly tacky and matte in color. Using a fine sieve, sprinkle some of the dusting mixture over the top of the marshmallow. Then run a sharp knife around the edge of your pan to loosen the marshmallow. Flip the pan over onto a cutting board and dust the exposed marshmallow with more coating powder.

Cut into squares, then toss with a bit more coating powder. Enjoy! Marshmallows are best stored in a cool, dry place. Store in an airtight container for 2 weeks and enjoy as a snack, in your hot cocoa, or toasted in an ooey, gooey s'more.

TIP: Marshmallows will continue to dry when exposed to air. For the perfect s'more, leave the freshly coated and cut marshmallows out for about an hour. This will allow them to better hold their shape and not melt *too* quickly when toasted.

blackberry-sage marshmallows

When I first started experimenting with marshmallows, I wanted to push the boundaries with flavors. Mixing fruit and herbs, sweet with savory or salty, and playing with new textures became a second hobby of mine. As we've grown, we've continued to play around with new combinations, but this one will forever have a special place in my heart. Blackberries have a mild sweetness to them, which complements the soft sage herb and the additional sweetness you get from the marshmallow. This flavor is always a hit when making s'mores and is a fun addition to a summer cocktail (Marshmallow Cocktails, page 148).
—KAT

2/3 cup fresh sage leaves

1½ cups granulated sugar

Unflavored nonstick pan spray

1 cup cold water, divided

3 tablespoons gelatin

1 cup corn syrup

2/3 cup blackberries, pureed, fresh or frozen

½ teaspoon kosher salt

2 to 3 drops of purple food coloring (optional)

Finely chop the sage leaves or pulse in the bowl of a food processor until slightly damp and light green. Mix with the sugar by hand until combined and fragrant. Set aside.

Prepare an 8 by 8-inch or 9 by 9-inch pan with a thin layer of unflavored nonstick pan spray. Set aside.

In a small microwave-safe bowl, pour ½ cup cold water and sprinkle the gelatin on top. Use a small whisk to combine and set aside. This process is called *blooming* the gelatin.

In a heavy-bottom 6 or 8-quart pan, combine the corn syrup, sage-infused sugar, remaining ½ cup water, blackberries, and salt. Cook over medium heat, occasionally swirling the pan until the sugar dissolves. After this point, do not stir or swirl the syrup in the pan.

Clip a candy thermometer to the pan and raise the temperature to high heat until the syrup reaches 240°F. This is known as the *soft ball stage* in candy making.

Once the syrup in the pan reaches 240°F, remove from heat and allow to cool to 220°F, then carefully pour into the bowl of the stand mixer.

continued

Heat the gelatin in the microwave on 50 percent power for 30-second intervals until liquid, between 1 and 2 minutes total. Then pour the gelatin mixture into the bowl of your stand mixer fitted with the whisk attachment. This is a good time to run your saucepan to the sink and soak with warm, soapy water.

Increase the mixer speed to medium for 3 to 5 minutes, allowing the mixture to become frothy and lighten in color. Then increase the speed to high for about 10 minutes until the mixture is thick and glossy. Add the food coloring, if using. You will know the marshmallow is ready when it has tripled in volume and starts to "pull" away from the edges of the bowl.

Working quickly, pour the marshmallow from the bowl into the prepared pan. Spread out into an even layer. Let rest for at least 4 hours, uncovered, at room temperature. Meanwhile, in a small bowl, mix one part cornstarch with three parts confectioners' sugar for dusting. This is called *coating powder.*

When the marshmallows are set, they will be slightly tacky and matte in color. Using a fine sieve, sprinkle some of the dusting mixture over the top of the marshmallow. Then run a sharp knife around the edge of your pan to loosen the marshmallow. Flip the pan over onto a cutting board and dust the exposed marshmallow with more coating powder.

Cut into squares, then toss with a bit more coating powder. Enjoy!

Marshmallows are best stored in a cool, dry place. Store in an airtight container for 2 weeks and enjoy as a snack, in your hot cocoa, or toasted in an ooey, gooey s'more.

TIP: Marshmallows will continue to dry when exposed to air. For the perfect s'more, leave the freshly coated and cut marshmallows out for about an hour. This will allow them to better hold their shape and not melt *too* quickly when toasted.

NOTE: If using fresh blackberries, make sure to push the puree through a sieve to remove the seeds.

VARIATIONS

strawberry-mint marshmallows

Swap out the pureed blackberries for strawberries and swap the sage for mint. Adding a few drops of red food coloring is optional. These marshmallows are perfect for topping mojitos.

blueberry-elderflower marshmallows

Replace the blackberry with blueberry puree. Omit the herbs. Replace 2 tablespoons of water in the syrup stage with 2 tablespoons of elderflower syrup. Adding a few drops of blue food coloring is optional.

tart cherry marshmallows

Replace the blackberries with tart cherries. Add 1 teaspoon of citric acid to the stand mixer after adding the gelatin and syrup. Add ½ teaspoon of almond extract at the final stage of whipping. Adding a few drops of red food coloring is optional.

champagne marshmallows

When Lindzi and I first met, she asked if I wanted to sell my gourmet marshmallows in her pop-up shop. We came up with an exclusive flavor that combined both of our personalities and brands—Champagne Marshmallows. We used a South African sparkling wine along with some gold sprinkles to create this memorable treat.

In this recipe, you simply replace the water with sparkling wine! We found that a dry champagne that has been opened and left flat works best for marshmallow making. The more subtle notes in the champagne tend to come forward in the marshmallows, so look for bubbles that have fruity or floral notes.
—KAT

Unflavored nonstick pan spray

1 cup cold champagne, divided

3 tablespoons gelatin

1 cup corn syrup

1½ cups granulated sugar

½ teaspoon kosher salt

Edible gold sprinkles or glitter dust (optional)

1 teaspoon vodka (optional)

Cornstarch or tapioca starch, for dusting

Confectioners' sugar, for dusting

Prepare an 8 by 8-inch or 9 by 9-inch pan with a thin layer of unflavored nonstick pan spray. Set aside.

In a small microwave-safe bowl, pour ½ cup cold champagne and sprinkle the gelatin on top. Use a small whisk to combine and set aside. This process is called *blooming* the gelatin.

In a heavy-bottom 6 or 8-quart pan, combine the corn syrup, sugar, remaining ½ cup champagne, and salt. Cook over medium heat, occasionally swirling the pan until the sugar dissolves. After this point, do not stir or swirl the syrup in the pan.

Clip a candy thermometer to the pan and raise the temperature to high heat until the syrup reaches 240°F. This is known as the *soft ball stage* in candy making.

Once the syrup in the pan reaches 240°F, remove from heat and allow to cool to 220°F, then carefully pour into the bowl of the stand mixer.

continued

Heat the gelatin in the microwave on 50 percent power for 30-second intervals until liquid, between 1 and 2 minutes total. Then pour the gelatin mixture into the bowl of your stand mixer fitted with the whisk attachment. This is a good time to run your saucepan to the sink and soak with warm, soapy water.

Increase the mixer speed to medium for 3 to 5 minutes, allowing the mixture to become frothy and lighten in color. Then increase the speed to high for about 10 minutes until the mixture is thick and glossy. You will know the marshmallow is ready when it has tripled in volume and starts to "pull" away from the edges of the bowl. If adding sprinkles, do so by hand in the last minute of mixing.

Working quickly, pour the marshmallow from the bowl into the prepared pan. Spread out into an even layer. Let rest for at least 4 hours, uncovered, at room temperature. Meanwhile, in a small bowl, mix one part cornstarch with three parts confectioners' sugar for dusting. This is called coating powder.

When the marshmallows are set, they will be slightly tacky and matte in color. If adding edible glitter, do so by mixing the glitter with 1 teaspoon of vodka. Then use a pastry brush to gently brush the glitter across the top of the marshmallows. Allow to dry for 1 to 2 minutes before coating.

Using a fine sieve, sprinkle some of the dusting mixture over the top of the marshmallow. Then run a sharp knife around the edge of your pan to loosen the marshmallow. Flip the pan over onto a cutting board and dust the exposed marshmallow with more coating powder.

Cut into squares, then toss with a bit more coating powder. Enjoy! Marshmallows are best stored in a cool, dry place. Store in an airtight container for 2 weeks and enjoy as a snack, in your hot cocoa, or toasted in an ooey, gooey s'more.

TIP: Marshmallows will continue to dry when exposed to air. For the perfect s'more, leave the freshly coated and cut marshmallows out for about an hour. This will allow them to better hold their shape and not melt too quickly when toasted.

boozy marshmallows

You may notice that marshmallows with alcohol tend to be denser or flat. This is because of how the alcohol interacts with the overall water in the recipe. In some cases, like with Champagne Marshmallows (page 40) or Kahlúa Marshmallows (page 29), you can replace some or all of the water with the liqueur. If you want to try making bourbon marshmallows, or tequila-infused marshmallows, substitute 2 tablespoons of cold water for alcohol before mixing with the gelatin.

layered marshmallows

Get creative with your flavors by layering them together!

Simply prepare two 8 by 8-inch or 9 by 9-inch pans with a thin layer of unflavored nonstick pan spray and spread half of the marshmallow batter into each pan. Repeat with your second flavor.

Slightly under-whip the marshmallow to easily pour each layer into the pan. For an even more precise method, weigh each pan as you go to ensure even distribution.

Do not add coating between the layers. Instead, add coating to the top of the final layer and let rest.

SUGGESTED FLAVOR COMBINATIONS

caramel macchiato marshmallows

One layer of Coffee Marshmallows (page 27), one layer of Salted-Caramel Marshmallows (page 33).

mimosa marshmallows

One layer of Champagne Marshmallows (page 40), one layer of Orange Marshmallows. Simply swap out 1 cup of water in the Vanilla Marshmallows (page 18) for pulp-free orange juice, or substitute orange extract for the vanilla extract.

banana cream pie marshmallows

One layer of Banana Cream Pie Marshmallows. Swap out the vanilla extract for banana extract in the Vanilla Marshmallows (page 18) and add a few drops of yellow food coloring. Followed by one layer of Vanilla Marshmallows. Top with crushed Gluten-Free Graham Crackers (page 57).

rainbow sherbet marshmallows

This flavor is easy to make as a layered marshmallow! To make your own rainbow sherbet extract, mix equal parts strawberry, orange, and lime extract in a small dish (about 2 tablespoons total). Prepare Vanilla Marshmallows (page 18), but instead of vanilla extract, add in the homemade rainbow sherbet extract. Working quickly, divide the whipped marshmallow into three bowls. Add 2 to 3 drops of orange food coloring to the first bowl, red food coloring to the second, and green food coloring to the third. Layer in the prepared pan and follow the rest of the recipe.

mango-habanero marshmallows

It's a funny story now, but a few years ago, my family did not find my first batch of these marshmallows so amusing—it was almost my last! Not having experience with using powdered peppers, I figured it would be easiest to throw a healthy amount (about a tablespoon or so) into the syrup stage of my marshmallows. Within a few minutes, my kitchen filled with a gaseous odor, and my eyes began to sting. Not realizing where it was coming from, I stepped into the living room and began to cough. Then my sister began to cough, and pretty soon everyone had itchy eyes. I think it was my dad who ran back into the kitchen, tossed the pot in the sink, and threw open all the doors and windows. I had succeeded in making habanero gas. Excellent.

Since then, I have learned quite a bit about using the right ingredients at the right moments—oh, and giving everyone fair warning before I start messing with new flavors. In this recipe, we use mango, which can be found fresh or as "mango pulp" in some freezer aisles at the grocery store. The coolness of the ripe fruit adds a balance to the heat.

You'll notice the amount of habanero powder has a range: 1/8 teaspoon is a mild heat that blends well with the mango, allowing both to shine; 1/4 teaspoon is for those who like it HOT. And, for the love of all marshmallow making, do NOT add the spice to the syrup stage—please add it like you would an extract—at the end! —KAT

Unflavored nonstick pan spray

1 cup cold water, divided

3 tablespoons gelatin

2/3 cup mango, pureed, fresh or frozen

1 cup corn syrup

1 1/2 cups sugar

1/2 teaspoon kosher salt

1/8 to 1/4 teaspoon habanero powder

2 to 3 drops of yellow food coloring (optional)

Cornstarch or tapioca starch, for dusting

Confectioners' sugar, for dusting

continued

Prep an 8 by 8-inch or 9 by 9-inch pan with a thin layer of unflavored nonstick pan spray. Set aside.

In a small microwave-safe bowl, pour ½ cup cold water and sprinkle the gelatin on top. Use a small whisk to combine and set aside. This process is called *blooming* the gelatin.

In a large heavy-bottom pan (10 or 12-quart) combine the mango, corn syrup, sugar, remaining ½ cup water, and salt. Cook over medium heat, occasionally swirling the pan until the sugar dissolves. After this point, do not stir or swirl the syrup in the pan. The mixture may bubble and climb up the size of the pot. This is normal.

Clip a candy thermometer into the pan and raise the temperature to high heat until the syrup reaches 240°F. This is known as the *soft ball stage* in candy making.

Once the syrup in the pan reaches 240°F, remove from heat and allow to cool to 220°F, then carefully pour into the bowl of the stand mixer.

Heat the gelatin in the microwave on 50 percent power for 30-second intervals until liquid, between 1 and 2 minutes total. Then pour the gelatin mixture into the bowl of your stand mixer fitted with the whisk attachment.

Turn the mixer on low and allow the syrup to combine with the gelatin. This is a good time to run your saucepan to the sink and soak with warm, soapy water.

Increase the mixer speed to medium for 3 to 5 minutes, allowing the mixture to become frothy and lighten in color. Then increase the speed to high for about 10 minutes until the mixture is thick and glossy. Add the habanero powder—⅛ teaspoon will give you a sweet heat, and ¼ teaspoon will yield a much hotter marshmallow. Add the 2 to 3 drops of yellow food coloring, if using. You will know the marshmallow is ready when it has tripled in volume and starts to "pull" away from the edges of the bowl.

Working quickly, use a spatula to scoop the marshmallow from the bowl into the prepared pan. Spread out into an even layer. Let rest for at least 4 hours, uncovered, at room temperature.

Meanwhile, in a small bowl, mix one part cornstarch with three parts confectioners' sugar for dusting. This is called *coating powder*.

When the marshmallows are set, they will be slightly tacky and matte in color. Using a fine sieve, sprinkle some of the dusting mixture over the top of the marshmallow. Then run a sharp knife around the edge of your pan to loosen the marshmallow. Flip the pan over onto a cutting board and dust the exposed marshmallow with more coating powder.

Cut into squares, then toss with a bit more coating powder. Enjoy! Marshmallows are best stored in a cool, dry place. Store in an airtight container for 2 weeks and enjoy as a snack, in your hot cocoa, or toasted in an ooey, gooey s'more.

TIP: Marshmallows will continue to dry when exposed to air. For the perfect s'more, leave freshly coated and cut marshmallows out for about an hour. This will allow them to better hold their shape and not melt *too* quickly when toasted.

ooey marshmallow goodness (OMG)
aka vanilla marshmallow cream

MAKES 8 CUPS

Homemade marshmallow cream, creme, or, as we call it, Ooey Marshmallow Goodness (OMG) are all the same concept. That creamy, spreadable marshmallow has a special place in my heart, and I remember making fluffernutter sandwiches (marshmallow cream and peanut butter) well into my college years. However, it wasn't until much more recently that I realized how many ways you can use and enjoy marshmallow cream. Use it as a frosting (page 66), in a s'more, as a replacement for marshmallows in hot cocoa, or toasted as a meringue topping on your favorite dessert. —KAT

½ cup water

1 cup granulated sugar

1½ cup corn syrup

1 teaspoon kosher salt

¾ cup egg whites

1 teaspoon cream of tartar

1 tablespoon vanilla extract

Make sure your bowl is incredibly clean and dry. This is very important in order for the marshmallow cream to hold its shape.

In a heavy-bottom 6 or 8-quart saucepan over medium heat, add the water, sugar, corn syrup, and salt. Stir to combine using a heat-proof spatula, then stop stirring. Clip a candy thermometer to the side of the pot and increase the heat to high until the temperature reaches 240°F.

When the temperature reaches 235°F, add the egg whites and cream of tartar to the bowl of a stand mixer. Whip on medium speed using the whisk attachment until soft peaks form. You can test by stopping the mixer and lifting the whisk. The meringue should hold a peak shape for a few seconds before falling back into the bowl. If the egg whites are ready before the syrup, simply turn off the mixer until the syrup reaches the correct temperature.

Turn the mixer on low speed and slowly stream the syrup into the bowl, aiming for the space between the whisk and the bowl. Once completely added, turn the mixer to medium and then high, preventing the hot syrup from splashing out of the bowl.

Whip until thick and glossy, about 7 to 8 minutes. Add the vanilla extract and continue whipping until the bowl feels cool to the touch.

Use right away or store in an airtight container. We recommend keeping your homemade marshmallow cream in the refrigerator for up to 2 weeks.

VARIATIONS

lemon marshmallow cream

Replace the vanilla extract with 2 tablespoons of lemon extract and add a few drops of yellow food coloring in the last minute of whipping for a fresh summer marshmallow cream.

birthday cake marshmallow cream

Add 1 teaspoon butter extract to the marshmallow cream in the final stage. Hand-fold in ¼ cup of rainbow sprinkles and enjoy!

peppermint marshmallow cream

Replace the vanilla extract with 1 teaspoon peppermint extract and add a swirl of red food coloring for a holiday marshmallow cream. Scoop onto hot cocoa for a minty twist on a festive favorite.

3

marshmallow sidekicks & mix-ins

There are many ways to add variety to your marshmallows, and we call these mix-ins in the XO kitchen. Mix-ins can be as simple as crushed graham crackers, a sweet dessert sauce, or a ganache. We've included a few recipes to get you started. Refer back to this section when you are celebrating with marshmallows (page 115).

chocolate ganache

Chocolate ganache always sounded so sophisticated and, therefore, difficult to make. But, once again, this is a recipe so simple and forgiving that I believe you can master it in no time. The main thing to note is that ganache is a ratio. Here, it is a 1:1 ratio of heavy cream and chocolate, meaning equal amounts of both ingredients. If you added more heavy cream (say, a 3:1 ratio of cream to chocolate), you would end up with a smoother, lighter ganache perfect for whipping. If you add more chocolate to cream (a 1:2 ratio of cream to chocolate), you will have a thicker, more stable ganache, typically used for making truffles or adding a drip effect to a cake. Either way, the process is the same! Simply heat the cream, pour over the chocolate, let sit, then stir. Easy peasy. **—KAT**

1½ cups chocolate, semisweet or bittersweet

1 cup heavy cream

Prep the chocolate by roughly chopping it and adding to a large glass bowl. Set aside.

Pour the cream into a heavy-bottom saucepan and heat over medium heat. The goal here is to scald the cream, meaning you want to heat it just before boiling. You will know it is ready when the cream starts to climb up the sides of the saucepan and is consistently simmering.

Pour the cream over the chocolate and let sit for 3 to 5 minutes.

Starting in the center of the bowl, slowly whisk together the chocolate and cream. The mixture will come together; just keep stirring. That's it! You just made chocolate ganache.

Use right away or transfer to an airtight container and store in the refrigerator. Ganache will last about 2 weeks in the fridge, or up to 2 months in the freezer.

VARIATIONS

milk chocolate ganache

2:1 ratio of chocolate to cream

white chocolate ganache

3:1 ratio of chocolate to cream

ADDING FLAVOR: Stir in 1 tablespoon dark rum or your favorite liquor to the ganache at the end of the process. You can also add flavor by steeping ingredients into the cream (Lapsang Souchong Ganache, page 127).

uses

1. Spread warm ganache on a graham cracker, top with a marshmallow, and toast for the perfect s'more.
2. Dip half of your s'mores into the ganache and refrigerate or freeze until the chocolate is hardened for "frozen s'mores."
3. Use ganache as a base for your Dessert Fondue (page 131).
4. Cool the ganache in the fridge for about 10 minutes, then scoop into the bowl of a stand mixer. Whip for a few moments until light and fluffy. Use as a frosting for cupcakes or cake.

salted-caramel sauce

Confession—I had never made caramel sauce before embarking on my marshmallow-making journey. I come from a long line of microwave bakers who grew up in the era of Rice Krispies Treats, doctored boxed-cake mixes, and other fun leftovers of convenience cooking. Any television representation of making caramels included high-boiling sugars, burns, and a lot of cursing. I love caramel and almost all warm, toasty flavors, so I get it. High risk, high reward. Cut to me in early 2015, trembling near my heavy-bottom saucepan, decked out in my brother's old skateboard safety gear, slowly pouring heavy cream into the hot pot, waiting for it to engulf me. I remember thinking, *Oh, that's it? That wasn't so bad!* I ditched the elbow pads and came to realize that it's all a big misconception. Yes, you are working with very hot sugar, and you should always be careful, but making caramels and caramel sauce *actually isn't any scarier than making marshmallows themselves!*

If you're nervous, it's OK to wear oven mitts while adding the cream. I have even taken the pot off heat entirely for a few seconds while adding the cooler fats to the sugar base. Just make sure you are fully incorporating the cream into the caramel by whisking until smooth. Once you have the process down, have fun! There are many applications for caramel sauce and quite a few ways to jazz up this base recipe. Just remember to let the caramel cool completely before adding it to Salted-Caramel Marshmallows (page 33). —KAT

1 cup water

3¾ cups granulated sugar

¼ cup light corn syrup

½ quart heavy cream, at room temperature

2 tablespoons vanilla extract

1½ teaspoons kosher salt

Add the water, sugar, and corn syrup to a large heavy-bottom pot. Stir to combine. Stir over medium heat until the sugar is dissolved, then stop stirring.

Increase the heat to high and let come to a boil. The sugar syrup will turn light amber, taking approximately 7 to 8 minutes. Do not stir, but you can occasionally swirl the pan to evenly distribute the heat.

continued

As soon as the syrup is uniformly amber, decrease the heat to low. Slowly add the cream; be careful, as this is when caramel sauce tends to boil up. Once added, whisk slowly to incorporate.

Add the vanilla and salt and continue to whisk until smooth and combined. Allow to come to a boil for 1 to 2 minutes, then remove from the heat. As it cools, the sauce will continue to thicken.

Pour into a glass jar or a heat-proof container, leaving uncovered until completely cool. Use right away or store at room temperature for up to a month.

NOTE: Adjust the salt to your tasting but do not leave out completely! The salt in this recipe helps balance the sweet–a necessity in confections and in life. Remove a tablespoon of sauce and allow to cool to room temperature before tasting. You can stir in salt to the larger batch and repeat this process until you are satisfied.

VARIATIONS

salted butter caramel

This variation is great for layering in desserts, whereas the original recipe is perfect for mixing into marshmallows, topping ice cream, or stirring into your latte.

Add ½ cup of butter at the heavy cream stage and allow the mixture to boil for a few minutes longer to make a thicker sauce, which will harden more like taffy.

cinnamon caramel

Add 2 to 3 fresh cinnamon sticks to heavy cream, bringing to a simmer over medium heat, then removing from heat. Allow to cool to room temperature and remove the sticks. Proceed with the recipe. Alternatively, you can whisk in 2 teaspoons of ground cinnamon with the vanilla extract and salt.

tea-infused caramel

Heat the cream in a small saucepan over medium heat until it begins to simmer. Add 2 teabags or 2 teaspoons of your preferred tea to the heavy cream and remove from the heat. Allow to steep for at least 20 minutes or up to an hour, until the cream cools to room temperature. Remove the tea bags or strain through a sieve before using. We love Earl Grey caramel sauce.

gluten-free graham crackers

MAKES 24 CRACKERS

When we decided to open the XO Marshmallow Cafe in 2017, we knew we wanted to offer s'mores. At markets and events, we were often greeted by enthusiastic customers eager for gluten-free desserts. So, as we began developing the menu, we decided to keep the cafe gluten-free, which meant finding gluten-free graham crackers. At the time, gluten-free ingredients were difficult to find, let alone gluten-free graham crackers. Pretty quickly, we realized that we had to make graham crackers in-house ourselves. Traditional graham crackers are made with graham flour, a whole-wheat flour, but this recipe uses a gluten-free flour blend with xanthan gum to help bind all the ingredients together. If your gluten-free flour does not contain xanthan gum, add 2 teaspoons to your dry ingredients. —KAT

½ cup unsalted butter

½ cup packed dark-brown sugar

1½ tablespoons honey

1½ tablespoons molasses

1¼ teaspoons vanilla extract

2 cups 1:1 gluten-free flour, plus more for rolling

½ teaspoon salt

½ teaspoon ground cinnamon

2½ tablespoons water

Turbinado sugar (optional)

In the bowl of a stand mixer fitted with a paddle attachment, cream the butter and sugar on medium-high speed until smooth (about 5 minutes). Add the honey, molasses, and vanilla extract to the bowl and mix on low speed until just combined.

In a separate bowl, mix together the flour, salt and cinnamon until combined. Add to the mixing bowl 1 cup at a time. Mix until no flour is visible, at low speed, until just combined.

At this point, the mixture will stick to the paddle attachment. Slowly stream in the water to help thin out the batter so it is pliable. Remove the dough from the mixer and roll into a large ball.

Preheat the oven to 350°F. Line a full baking sheet with parchment paper. Alternatively, you can line two half baking sheets with parchment paper.

continued

On a lightly floured surface, roll the dough out to ¼-inch thickness. It may help to place between two pieces of parchment paper on your baking sheet and spread out evenly into the pan using a rolling pin or your hands. Once rolled, using a knife or cookie cutter, lightly indent the dough to create square or rectangular shapes, about 3 by 3 inches. If using, sprinkle the top of the graham crackers with coarse turbinado sugar; lightly press the sugar into the dough.

Bake for about 10 minutes, remove from the oven, and use a fork to add two rows of dots per cracker. Decrease the temperature to 300°F. Return to the oven for another 15 to 20 minutes or until the crackers are deep golden brown throughout. Remove from the oven. Repeat the indentations with a knife or cookie cutter to break the cookies apart.

Store in an airtight container for up to 2 weeks or until your next campout.

cinnamon sugar graham crackers

If you're looking for a graham cracker that is a little sweeter, look no further. The cinnamon sugar grahams give your s'mores a little something extra . . . and we are nothing if not extra.

½ cup unsalted butter

½ cup packed dark-brown sugar

1½ tablespoons honey

1½ tablespoons molasses

1¼ teaspoons vanilla extract

2 cups 1:1 gluten-free flour

½ teaspoon salt

1 teaspoon ground cinnamon, plus 1 tablespoon for topping

2½ tablespoons water

¼ cup granulated sugar, for topping

Turbinado sugar (optional)

In the bowl of a stand mixer fitted with a paddle attachment, cream the butter and sugar on medium-high speed until smooth (about 5 minutes). Add the honey, molasses, and vanilla extract to the bowl and mix on low speed until just combined.

In a separate bowl, mix together the flour, salt, and 1 teaspoon of the cinnamon until combined. Add to the mixing bowl, 1 cup at a time. Mix until no flour is visible, at low speed, until just combined.

At this point, the mixture will stick to the paddle attachment. Slowly stream in the water to help thin out the batter so it is pliable. Remove the dough from the mixer and roll into a large ball.

Preheat the oven to 350°F. Line a full baking sheet with parchment paper. Alternatively, you can line two half baking sheets with parchment paper.

On a lightly floured surface, roll the dough out to ¼-inch thickness. It may help to place between two pieces of parchment paper on your baking sheet and spread out evenly into the pan using a rolling pin or your hands. Once rolled, using a knife or cookie cutter, lightly indent the dough to create square or rectangular shapes, about 3 by 3 inches.

continued

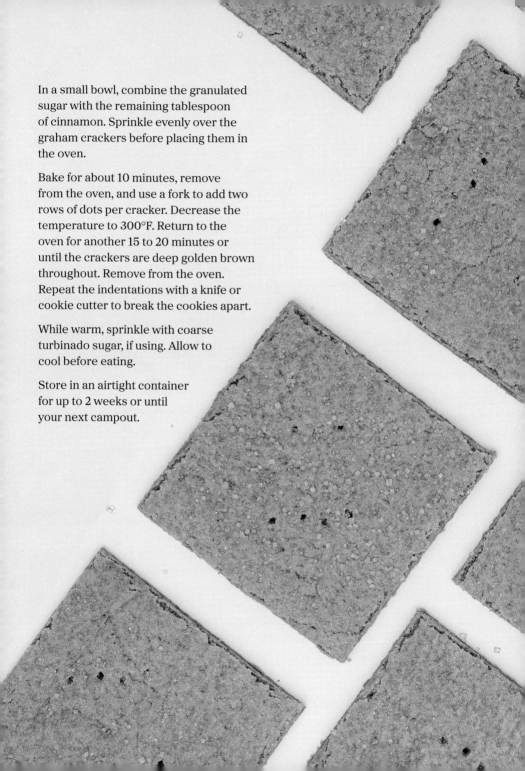

In a small bowl, combine the granulated sugar with the remaining tablespoon of cinnamon. Sprinkle evenly over the graham crackers before placing them in the oven.

Bake for about 10 minutes, remove from the oven, and use a fork to add two rows of dots per cracker. Decrease the temperature to 300°F. Return to the oven for another 15 to 20 minutes or until the crackers are deep golden brown throughout. Remove from the oven. Repeat the indentations with a knife or cookie cutter to break the cookies apart.

While warm, sprinkle with coarse turbinado sugar, if using. Allow to cool before eating.

Store in an airtight container for up to 2 weeks or until your next campout.

chocolate graham crackers

Not that we need an excuse to have chocolate, but these chocolate grahams completely satisfy our cravings. The bitter cocoa brings out the earthiness of the cracker, while a layer of sugar rounds out the flavor. Pair with a Coffee Marshmallow (page 27), or use as the base for a chocolate graham cracker crust!

½ cup unsalted butter

½ cup packed dark-brown sugar

1½ tablespoons honey

1½ tablespoons molasses

1¼ teaspoons vanilla extract

1¾ cups 1:1 gluten-free flour

½ cup cocoa powder

½ teaspoon salt

2½ tablespoons water

¼ cup granulated sugar, for topping

Turbinado sugar (optional)

In the bowl of a stand mixer fitted with a paddle attachment, cream the butter and sugar on medium-high speed until smooth (about 5 minutes). Add the honey, molasses, and vanilla extract to the bowl and mix on low speed until just combined.

In a separate bowl, mix together the flour, cocoa, and salt until combined. Add to the mixing bowl, 1 cup at a time. Mix until no flour is visible, at low speed, until just combined.

At this point, the mixture will stick to the paddle attachment. Slowly stream in the water to help thin out the batter so it is pliable. Remove the dough from the mixer and roll into a large ball.

Preheat the oven to 350°F. Line a full baking sheet with parchment paper. Alternatively, you can line two half baking sheets with parchment paper.

On a lightly floured surface, roll the dough out to ¼-inch thickness. It may help to place it between two pieces of parchment paper on your baking sheet and spread out evenly into the pan using a rolling pin or your hands. Once rolled, using a knife or cookie cutter, lightly indent the dough to create square or rectangular shapes, about 3 by 3 inches.

Bake for about 10 minutes, remove from the oven, and use a fork to add two rows of dots per cracker. Decrease the temperature to 300°F. Return to the oven for another 15 to 20 minutes or until the crackers are deep golden brown throughout. Remove from the oven. Repeat the indentations with a knife or cookie cutter to break cookies apart.

Store in an airtight container for up to 2 weeks or until your next campout.

graham cracker crust

OK, let's be honest here . . . cheesecake is better than pie. I said it. I love the contrast of toasty, dense crust with a smooth and cool filling. And, if you're like us and always on the go, this recipe for your own graham cracker crust will quickly elevate whatever you're making! We use it in our Sweet Potato Pie (page 134). This recipe can easily be doubled for a 9 by 13-inch dessert, or a 10-inch pan. —KAT

1¼ cups Gluten-Free Graham Crackers, crushed (page 57)

¼ cup granulated sugar

5 tablespoons unsalted butter, melted

Combine all the ingredients in a bowl, mixing until no large lumps remain.

Press evenly into an 8 or 9-inch pan.

FOR BAKED DESSERTS: Bake at 325°F for 5 to 7 minutes or until just golden brown. Let chill before filling.

FOR NO-BAKE DESSERTS: Chill the crust in the fridge for at least an hour before filling.

marshmallow frosting

Our marshmallow cream makes a beautiful filling for desserts. But sometimes you just want that silky-smooth American buttercream. We've been there. This recipe combines our marshmallow cream with a fluffy and very easy frosting base to make a sweet frosting perfect for your next batch of cupcakes, Whoopsie Pies (page 102), or our S'mores Cake (page 127). —KAT

1 cup unsalted butter, at room temperature

2 cups confectioners' sugar

4 cups Ooey Marshmallow Goodness (OMG) (page 48)

1 teaspoon vanilla extract

In the bowl of a stand mixer fitted with the paddle attachment, or using a hand mixer, whip together the butter and confectioners' sugar until noticeably light and fluffy. Start on low speed and increase to medium-high speed; this should take about 5 minutes. Hand-mix in the marshmallow cream and vanilla until incorporated.

The marshmallow frosting is ready to pipe but can also be chilled. The colder the frosting, the firmer it will become. Toast with a culinary torch for the ultimate campfire vibe.

VARIATION

toasted marshmallow frosting

Substitute the marshmallow cream with toasted marshmallows! Simply cut prepared marshmallows into small cubes and spread out on a baking sheet. Using a culinary torch, toast the marshmallows and let cool for a few minutes. Add to the frosting in the same step as the marshmallow cream.

4

making things with marshmallows

You've mastered the art of marshmallow making; now let's *make some things* with marshmallows! From brown butter cereal treats to truffles, from fudge to the perfect cup of hot cocoa, elevate your snacks with the addition of homemade marshmallows or marshmallow cream. The following recipes are some of our favorite recommendations, and we cannot wait until you make them your own.

s'mores 101: how to make the perfect s'more

Since we've started making gourmet marshmallows, we've been asked, "Are they good in s'mores?" And we can only say—YES. Yes, yes, yes. Our flavors are delicious on their own, but combined with various chocolates, graham crackers, and other fillings, they are nearly unstoppable. Below, find some of our signature s'mores, and don't be afraid to make your own unique creations!
—LINDZI

VARIATIONS

classic s'more

Lay two classic Gluten-Free Graham Crackers (page 57) on a plate. Add a square of milk or dark chocolate to one graham, then toast a Vanilla Marshmallow (page 18) over an open flame, rotating consistently to ensure it is heated evenly. Once the marshmallow is golden brown or completely burnt (no judgment!), place it on top of the chocolate and top with the other graham cracker, creating a sandwich. Lightly "smoosh" for a new summertime favorite!

salty & sweet s'more

Take a pretzel crisp and add a Ghirardelli caramel-filled chocolate square to the top of it. Alternatively, you can make this recipe with a square of dark chocolate and Salted-Caramel Sauce (page 54) drizzled on top. Then toast a Salted-Caramel Marshmallow (page 33) over an open flame, rotating consistently to ensure it is heated evenly. Once the marshmallow is golden brown, place it on top of the chocolate. Add a pinch of sea salt and top with the other pretzel crisp, creating a small sandwich. Lightly "smoosh" for a salty-sweet treat.

continued

tea party s'more

Lay two shortbread cookies on a plate.
Add a square of white chocolate to
one cookie. Then toast a Lavender–
Honey Marshmallow (page 22) over
an open flame, rotating consistently
to ensure it is heated evenly. Once
the marshmallow is golden brown or
completely burnt (no judgment!), place
it on top of the white chocolate. Drizzle
a little honey over the marshmallow
and top with the other shortbread
cookie. This s'more dazzles at a tea
party or displayed on a dessert table.
Leave un-"smooshed" for height.

spicy s'more

Lay two classic Gluten-Free Graham Crackers (page 57) on a plate. Add a square of milk
chocolate to one graham, followed with a slice of fresh mango. Then toast a Mango–
Habanero Marshmallow (page 45) over an open flame, rotating consistently to ensure
it is heated evenly. Once the marshmallow is golden brown or completely burnt (no
judgment!), place it on top of the chocolate and mango. Sprinkle with a hit of cayenne
pepper or Tajin seasoning, and top with the other graham cracker, creating a sandwich.
Lightly "smoosh" and enjoy the heat!

charcuterie s'more

A charcuterie s'more can be made of many ingredients, but our favorites include a
mixture of chocolates, marshmallows, and fruit. For example, pair Chocolate Graham
Crackers (page 62), a Coffee Marshmallow (page 27), and raspberries. Another favorite?
Cinnamon Sugar Graham Crackers (page 59), fresh brie, and strawberries. Looking for
an easy out-of-the-box combination? How about Gluten-Free Graham Crackers (page
57), Blackberry–Sage Marshmallows (page 36), and white chocolate?

the fluffernutter sandwich

MAKES 1 SANDWICH

Made with our Ooey Marshmallow Goodness (OMG) (page 48) and a healthy dollop of peanut butter or nut-free butter, the fluffernutter is a popular after-school treat made with marshmallow cream and peanut butter.

2 pieces white bread, toasted

1 to 2 tablespoons Ooey Marshmallow Goodness (OMG) (page 48)

1 tablespoon creamy peanut butter or other nut or nut-free butter

To make, simply toast two pieces of white bread, then add a thick layer of peanut butter (or your favorite nut or nut-free butter) to one slice and a generous scoop of marshmallow cream to the other. Finally, like Joey from *Friends,* "put your hands together."

the perfect cup of hot cocoa

MAKES 2 SERVINGS

From the first cocoa mix that paired with the first batch of gourmet marshmallows to the opening day of the cafe, our pursuit of creating the *perfect* cup of hot cocoa has been present since day one. Over time, we have found that everyone enjoys a cup of cocoa their own way, but our hot cocoa base is sure to please you and a crowd. The secret? Quality dark chocolate. The higher the quality, the richer the final cup will be. Making a larger batch for a larger group? No problem! Simply double or triple the recipe and keep warm by storing in a small slow cooker on low heat. —LINDZI

3 cups whole milk

¼ cup granulated sugar

⅓ cup unsweetened cocoa powder

8 ounces (1 cup) dark chocolate, chopped or chips

¼ teaspoon vanilla extract or ¼ teaspoon ground cinnamon (optional)

4 Vanilla Marshmallows (page 18)

In a small saucepan, add the whole milk, sugar, and cocoa powder. Whisk slowly on medium-low heat until the sugar and cocoa powder have dissolved. Then slowly stir until the mixture is simmering, not boiling.

Add the dark chocolate and stir until evenly distributed.

Remove from heat and stir in vanilla extract or ground cinnamon, if using.

Top with two Vanilla Marshmallows before serving. Enjoy!

NOTE: You may substitute whole milk for nonfat milk or another alternative milk, but your cocoa may thin as a result. When adding the dark chocolate, consider adding another ounce to the mix to yield a lovely, rich cup of hot cocoa.

marshmallow
fudge

My mom made a version of fudge using the microwave and just a couple of ingredients. Though delicious (and often messy), the fudge was best served immediately and did not freeze or thaw well. I found that with the addition of a few more ingredients, including marshmallows, you'll end up with a much richer batch of yummy fudge.

The key to making fudge is all about the timing. For this recipe, it is important to lay out all ingredients premeasured and ready to go. **—KAT**

Unflavored nonstick pan spray

¾ cup unsalted butter

2¾ cups granulated sugar

⅔ cup evaporated milk

¼ teaspoon kosher salt, plus more for sprinkling

1 cup Ooey Marshmallow Goodness (OMG) (page 48)

2 cups bittersweet chocolate (the higher the quality, the better)

1 teaspoon vanilla extract

1 cup roughly chopped nuts, like walnuts or pistachios (optional)

Line an 8 by 8-inch or 9 by 9-inch pan with parchment paper and unflavored nonstick pan spray. Set aside.

In a heavy-bottom 8-quart saucepan, combine the butter, sugar, evaporated milk, and ¼ teaspoon of salt over medium heat. Stir constantly until the mixture begins to bubble (about 7 minutes). Clip a candy thermometer to the side of the pan.

Continue to stir until the mixture reaches 234°F. Once the temperature is reached, remove from the stove immediately to stop cooking.

Working quickly, stir in the marshmallow cream, chocolate, vanilla, and nuts, if using. Once all the ingredients are incorporated, pour into the prepared pan. Sprinkle some kosher salt on top for an extra-salty bite! Let cool completely, at least 4 hours.

Cut into 36 small (1-inch) squares or 12 large (3-inch) squares and enjoy!

NOTE: Homemade fudge will last about a week at room temperature, between 2 and 3 weeks if kept in the refrigerator, or up to 3 months if stored in an airtight container in the freezer. Let the fudge come to room temperature on the counter before serving.

TIP: You can easily swap the marshmallow cream in this recipe for marshmallows! Melt 2 cups marshmallows with 1 tablespoon of butter and proceed with the rest of the recipe.

classic chocolate truffles

MAKES 12 LARGE OR 24 SMALL TRUFFLES

When my mother and I would go for a girls' girl day of shopping, we would always make a stop for some truffles. No lady's day out was complete without this decadent treat. The tradition of each picking out a single chocolate truffle started with her mother and has carried on with the women in my family ever since. Now, I find a lot of joy in making homemade chocolate truffles, and because you have already mastered the art of Chocolate Ganache (page 52), I know you'll be an expert soon enough! From our base recipe, you can customize your confections with different coatings or mix-ins. Below, you'll find some of our favorite ways to incorporate marshmallowy goodness into every bite and to share with the special people in your life. **—KAT**

1½ cups semisweet chocolate chips

⅔ cup heavy cream

1 tablespoon unsalted butter, at room temperature

½ teaspoon vanilla extract

Cocoa powder, chopped nuts, chocolate coating, edible glitter, or sprinkles, for topping

Add the chocolate to a medium bowl.

In a heavy-bottom pan, bring the heavy cream to a simmer over medium-low heat. The cream will start to bubble and rise up the edges of the pan. Do not walk away during this stage or your cream will surely boil over the pan. Trust us!

Add the butter to the cream and pour the heated cream over the chocolate chips, making sure the chips are submerged and evenly coated. Allow to sit for 3 minutes.

Add the vanilla extract and use a whisk to slowly stir. The mixture will start coming together in the middle and is done when the entire mixture is a silky, pourable chocolate sauce consistency.

Cover the bowl with plastic wrap, pressing the wrap to touch the top of the ganache. Chill for 1 hour in the fridge.

continued

Line a baking sheet with parchment paper. Use a tablespoon or small cookie scoop to spoon a tablespoon at a time onto the parchment paper. If you'd like, you can roll the ganache into uniform ball shapes before setting on the parchment paper. Once all the balls have been rolled, place back in the fridge while preparing your toppings.

Once firm and chilled, roll the truffles in cocoa powder, nuts, chocolate coating, edible glitter, or sprinkles!

These truffles can get soft if left out too long, so store in the fridge until ready to serve, up to 2 weeks.

VARIATION

boozy truffles

Replace the vanilla extract in the Classic Chocolate Truffles (page 79) recipe with your favorite rum, cognac, or bourbon. Keep the rest of the steps the same. We love to decorate these differently so that guests know which truffles contain alcohol.

s'mores truffles

1¼ cups crushed Gluten-Free Graham Crackers (page 57), divided

1 cup semisweet chocolate chips

¼ teaspoon kosher salt

2 cups Ooey Marshmallow Goodness (OMG) (page 48)

1 cup melting chocolate, dark or milk, for dipping

¼ cup crushed grahams, for finishing

In a medium bowl, combine 1 cup crushed graham crackers, chocolate chips, salt, and marshmallow cream. Mix until well combined.

Line a baking sheet with parchment or wax paper.

Use a tablespoon or small cookie scoop to roll the mixture into uniform balls roughly the size of 1 tablespoon. Place on the parchment paper and freeze for 15 minutes, or keep in the fridge until ready to dip.

Prepare the melting chocolate according to directions. Alternatively, in a small bowl, melt 1 cup chocolate chips with ¼ cup vegetable or coconut oil. Stir until smooth and combined.

Pour the remaining ¼ cup of crushed grahams into a shallow bowl or onto a plate.

Use a fork to dip each s'mores ball into chocolate and then roll in the bowl of crushed grahams. Line back up on the baking sheet and chill until set (about 45 minutes).

Store truffles in the fridge until ready to serve. They will last about 2 weeks if refrigerated in an airtight container.

chocolate chip cookie dough truffles

MAKES 12 LARGE OR 24 SMALL TRUFFLES

½ cup all-purpose or gluten-free flour

½ cup unsalted butter

¾ cup packed dark-brown sugar

1 teaspoon vanilla extract

1 teaspoon kosher salt

1 cup mini semisweet chocolate chips

1 cup Ooey Marshmallow Goodness (OMG) (page 48)

Melting chocolate, for dipping

Mini semisweet chocolate chips, to finish

To heat-treat your flour: preheat the oven to 300°F and spread the flour onto a baking sheet in a thin layer. Bake for about 10 minutes. Remove from the oven and allow to cool. This process will kill all bacteria and make the raw cookie dough safe for consumption.

In a bowl with a hand mixer, or in the bowl of a stand mixer fitted with the paddle attachment, cream together the butter and brown sugar until light and fluffy. Start on low speed to incorporate the ingredients, and raise to high speed after about a minute. You will know it is ready when the mixture is smooth and a very light-tan color (5 to 7 minutes). Add the vanilla and mix until combined.

Add the flour, salt, and mini chocolate chips. Mix until well combined. Add the marshmallow cream and combine by hand until evenly distributed.

Scoop into tablespoon-size balls and place on a baking sheet lined with parchment paper. Chill for at least 30 minutes in the fridge to make dipping them easier.

Prepare the melting chocolate according to directions. Alternatively, in a small bowl, melt 1 cup chocolate chips with ¼ cup vegetable or coconut oil. Stir until smooth and combined.

Pour the mini chocolate chips into a shallow bowl or onto a plate.

Use a fork to dip each s'mores ball into chocolate, and then roll in the bowl of prepared chocolate chips. Line back up on the baking sheet and chill until set (about 45 minutes).

Store truffles in the fridge until ready to serve. They will last about 2 weeks if refrigerated in an airtight container.

VARIATION
sugar cookie dough truffles

Follow the instructions for the Chocolate Chip Cookie Dough Truffles (page 82), but swap the chocolate chips with nonpareil sprinkles. Use while melting the chocolate, and top with additional nonpareil sprinkles.

s'mores pop pastries (two ways)

MAKES 3 POP PASTRIES

I grew up with a pretty typical '90s kid breakfast—mostly cereal, the occasional granola bar—but when my sisters and I were really, really lucky, we got Pop-Tarts. There was always a fight over what Pop-Tarts flavor would grace our house. One sister wanted cherry, one wanted wild berry, and I always wanted brown sugar cinnamon—but there was one flavor that we could always agree on: s'mores. The debate whether it was better heated up or cold is still one we cannot agree on to this day (heated up is the only correct choice). I figured if there was any way to get others on my side of the debate, I'd just have to create the perfect s'more pop pastries. The main thing I felt could always be better? More marshmallow! —LINDZI

for both pop pastries

2 sheets prepared puff pastry, thawed

1 cup Chocolate Ganache (page 52)

2 cups Vanilla Marshmallows (page 18) or Ooey Marshmallow Goodness (OMG) (page 48)

1 large egg, beaten

Crushed Gluten-Free Graham Crackers (page 57), for topping

continued

VARIATIONS

marshmallow-stuffed pop pastries

Preheat the oven to 375°F or the temperature recommended on the prepared pastry box.

Roll out the pastry and cut into even rectangles or squares, approximately 3 by 4 inches. You will end up with about six squares.

Using a spatula, spread a layer of chocolate ganache across the top of half of the pastry squares, leaving about a ¼-inch border around all sides.

Using another spatula, spread a layer of marshmallow cream across the top of the remaining half of the pastry squares, leaving about a ¼-inch border around all sides. Alternatively, you can add two Vanilla Marshmallows (page 18) in lieu of marshmallow cream.

Flip the marshmallow-covered pastry on top of the chocolate-covered pastry square so the fillings are on the inside. Use your fingers to pinch together the border.

Use a fork to crimp the sides all around the edges of the pastry. Poke a few holes in the top for ventilation.

Prepare two baking sheets with parchment paper. Place each prepared pastry onto the baking sheets and brush with the beaten egg to create an "egg wash."

Bake for approximately 10 to 12 minutes, or until the edges are golden brown and the pastry is slightly golden. Remove from the oven and allow to cool.

Once cool, spread additional Chocolate Ganache (page 52) on the top and sprinkle with the crushed grahams.

These breakfast-y treats are best served immediately but will last another day if stored in an airtight container overnight.

marshmallow-topped pop pastries

Follow the above recipe but omit the marshmallow cream from the filling. Instead, double the amount of ganache filling by spreading it on all the pastry halves. Add a sprinkle of crushed graham crackers over the filling. Proceed with the recipe.

Once the pastry has cooled completely, use a sandwich bag or piping bag to pipe a squiggle of marshmallow cream onto each pop pastry. Use a culinary torch to toast each pop pastry.

These topped treats are best served immediately but will last another day if stored in an airtight container overnight. Simply wait to top with marshmallow cream until ready to serve.

marshmallow dream bars

We both agree that we absolutely love rice crispy cereal treats. However, we have a tendency to disagree on how we like our texture. Lindzi prefers a gooier treat with extra marshmallow, and Kat loves a slightly crispier treat with the perfect amount of chewiness. When it came time to create a cereal treat for our cafe (what we call our Marshmallow Dream Bars), we were up to the challenge of creating a treat that would indulge both of our tastes. After lots of delicious trial and error, we created the ultimate Marshmallow Dream Bar. It's loaded with lots of ooey, gooey marshmallows that easily pull apart, but the cereal itself is perfectly crispy for an additional crunch. The biggest secret to this treat that makes us both grab at any chance to eat them? Browned butter. Trust us. —KAT AND LINDZI

10 ounces (about half a batch) Vanilla Marshmallows (page 18), cut into rough pieces

Unflavored nonstick pan spray

¼ cup unsalted butter

1 teaspoon kosher salt

1 teaspoon vanilla extract

6 cups crispy rice cereal

Roughly chop the marshmallows and lay them out on a plate to dry (at least 30 minutes, or overnight for best results). Then spray an 8 by 8-inch pan with unflavored nonstick pan spray and set aside.

In a large pot, melt the butter over medium-low heat. Stir frequently, allowing the butter to become golden brown and nutty, about 5 minutes. Do not walk away because butter can go from browned to burnt in a flash.

When the butter has browned, remove from the heat. Add the marshmallows to the pot; stir until almost completely melted. Add the salt and vanilla; stir to combine.

Moving quickly, add the cereal to the pot and coat with the butter–marshmallow mixture. Make sure the cereal is fully coated and no mixture is stuck to the bottom of the pan.

continued

Pour into the prepared pan, using your hands with a bit of unflavored nonstick pan spray (or butter) to smooth out the treats.

Let cool. When ready to serve, cut into squares. Treats will last up to 5 days if kept at room temperature in an airtight container.

VARIATION

s'mores cereal treats

One of our favorite things about this recipe is that you're not limited to just a classic rice crispy cereal treat. Mix it up! You can easily swap out different cereals or marshmallow flavors to create some fantastic combinations.

Prepare the Marshmallow Dream Bars (page 87) and fold in by hand ¼ cup Chocolate Ganache (page 52) and ¼ cup crushed Gluten-Free Graham Crackers (page 57) when adding the vanilla extract and salt. You can also decorate with a drizzle of chocolate and a sprinkle of additional crushed graham crackers, if you like.

sherbirthday cereal treats

- 10 ounces (about half a batch) Vanilla Marshmallows (page 18), cut into rough pieces
- Unflavored nonstick pan spray
- ¼ cup unsalted butter
- 1 teaspoon kosher salt
- ¼ teaspoon strawberry or raspberry extract
- ¼ teaspoon orange extract
- ¼ teaspoon lime extract
- 2 to 3 drops orange food coloring (optional)
- 6 cups Fruity Pebbles cereal

Roughly chop the marshmallows and lay them out on a plate to dry (at least 30 minutes, or overnight for best results). Then spray an 8 by 8-inch pan with unflavored nonstick pan spray and set aside.

In a large pot, over medium-low heat, melt the butter. Stir frequently, allowing the butter to become golden brown and nutty, about 5 minutes. Do not walk away! Butter can go from browned to burnt in a flash if you look away.

When the butter has browned, remove from the heat. Add the marshmallows to the pot; stir until almost completely melted. Add the salt, extracts, and food coloring, if using. Stir to combine.

Moving quickly, add the cereal to the pot and coat with the butter–marshmallow mixture. Make sure the cereal is fully coated and no mixture is stuck to the bottom of the pan.

Pour the treats into the prepared pan, using your hands with a bit of unflavored nonstick pan spray (or butter) to smooth out the treats.

Let cool. When ready to serve, cut into squares. Treats will last up to 5 days if kept at room temperature in an airtight container.

cinnamon toast dream bars

10 ounces (about half a batch) Vanilla Marshmallows (page 18)

Unflavored nonstick pan spray

¼ cup unsalted butter

1 teaspoon kosher salt

½ teaspoon maple extract

¼ teaspoon ground cinnamon

6 cups Cinnamon Toast Crunch cereal

Roughly chop the marshmallows and lay them out on a plate to dry for at least 30 minutes (or overnight for best results). Then spray an 8 by 8-inch pan with unflavored nonstick pan spray and set aside.

In a large pot, over medium-low heat, melt the butter. Stir frequently, allowing the butter to become golden brown and nutty, about 5 minutes. Do not walk away! Butter can go from browned to burnt in a flash if you look away.

When the butter has browned, remove from the heat. Add the marshmallows to the pot and stir until almost completely melted. Add the kosher salt, maple extract, and ground cinnamon. Stir to combine.

Moving quickly, add the cereal to the pot and coat with the butter–marshmallow mixture. Make sure the cereal is fully coated and that none of the mixture is stuck to the bottom of the pan.

Pour the treats into the prepared pan, coating your hands with a bit of unflavored nonstick pan spray (or butter) to smooth out the treats.

Let cool. When ready to serve, cut into squares. Treats will last up to 5 days if kept at room temperature in an airtight container.

antonia's puppy chow mix

I think I started the Great Chocolate Fight of 1994. I have a very specific memory of my mother and me in the kitchen together. I was about four or five years old, and I sat on the counter as my mom melted some chocolate chips and peanut butter in the microwave. What felt like a giant bowl of cereal sat next to me, and I was eager to help shake, shake, shake—my favorite part of making puppy chow. I also loved the name of it but never quite understood why this delicious snack was likened to dog food.

The microwave beeped, and Mom carefully moved the melty chocolate mix to the counter, where she stirred the last bits of chocolate chips. I grabbed the flat rubber edge of the spatula, getting chocolate all over my toddler hands. Mom laughed, so I laughed, and as she came closer with a wet paper towel, I impulsively dotted her cheek with a big chocolate fingerprint. I am not sure what happened next, but I remember my father coming home to a kitchen absolutely devastated in chocolate. No puppy chow was made that day. Now, anytime I make this yummy dessert, I think of that messy afternoon with my mom, Antonia. —KAT

6 cups Chex or Crispix cereal

1 (12-ounce) bag semisweet chocolate chips

1 cup creamy peanut butter or other nut butter

¼ cup unsalted butter

1 teaspoon vanilla extract

A pinch of kosher salt

4 to 6 cups confectioners' sugar

Make sure to measure out all the ingredients before starting. This is a quick process, and you want to be able to move quickly through it.

Pour the cereal into a large bowl, set aside.

In a medium microwave-safe bowl, add the chocolate chips, peanut butter, and butter. Heat at 50 percent power in the microwave for 1 minute and stir. Then heat in 30-second increments until the mixture is fully melted and combined. Add the vanilla extract and salt.

Quickly pour the chocolate mixture over the cereal and stir to coat the cereal completely.

continued

Transfer the mixture to a large paper bag and add 4 cups of the confectioners' sugar. Tightly roll the bag and shake vigorously to combine. You want the powdered sugar to adhere to the cereal before it is completely cooled. Add more powdered sugar, ½ cup at a time, until the cereal is evenly coated and a light-gray color.

Transfer the puppy chow to an airtight container and chill in the refrigerator for at least an hour. Enjoy chilled or at room temperature (this is a hotly debated topic). Puppy chow will last at least a week at room temperature and about 2 weeks in the refrigerator.

NOTES: Swap out the peanut butter for your favorite nut butter or sunflower butter for a nut-free alternative. Keep in mind that most organic butters contain more fat, so adjust the unsalted butter as needed. To make this vegan, swap the butter for vegan butter.

You can also swap out the vanilla extract for maple syrup or other flavored extracts.

We like using semisweet chocolate to balance the sweetness of the powdered sugar, but you can easily substitute milk chocolate or white chocolate for a brighter, sweeter, treat.

not your '90s oatmeal cream pies

MAKES 12 PIES

When people talk about the '90s, people often reference the fashion (so much denim) and the iconic TV shows (*Are You Afraid of the Dark?*, anyone?!), but I always think of the snacks. I'm a true '90s baby through and through—from Gushers to Mondo drinks to anything Little Debbie, it was part of my snack rotation. One of my go-to favorites was Oatmeal Creme Pies, with the chewy cookies, the creamy filling—I loved it all. Not too long ago, I was craving an Oatmeal Creme Pie and wanted to play around with the idea of making my own with a marshmallow twist. Luckily, I had a pint of our Ooey Marshmallow Goodness (OMG) (page 48) in my fridge, so all I had to do was make some cookies, fill it with marshmallow cream, and enjoy while trying to find one of my favorite '90s cartoons streaming. But don't worry, you don't have to be a '90s baby to enjoy this recipe (but I do secretly think it makes them better somehow). **—LINDZI**

cookies

1½ cups old-fashioned rolled oats

¾ cup all-purpose flour or gluten-free flour

1 teaspoon ground cinnamon

½ teaspoon baking powder

½ teaspoon kosher salt

¼ teaspoon baking soda

½ cup salted butter, at room temperature

½ cup packed dark-brown sugar

½ cup granulated sugar

1 large egg

1 teaspoon vanilla extract

⅛ teaspoon maple extract (optional)

filling

About 1½ cups Ooey Marshmallow Goodness (OMG) (page 48) or Marshmallow Frosting (page 66)

continued

To make the cookies, preheat the oven to 350°F. Line two baking sheets with parchment paper.

In a medium bowl, whisk together the oats, flour, cinnamon, baking powder, salt, and baking soda. Set aside.

Cream the butter and sugars together in the bowl of a stand mixer fitted with the paddle attachment on medium speed until light and fluffy, about 3 minutes. Add the egg and vanilla extract, and maple extract, if using. Still at medium speed, beat until combined.

Next, stop the mixer to add the flour mixture to the bowl. On low speed, mix until completely incorporated and no visible flour remains, about 1 minute.

Using a 2-tablespoon scoop, scoop the dough onto the prepared baking sheets, spacing each scoop 2 inches apart.

Bake your cookies on your upper and lower oven racks until the cookies are golden brown, 10 to 12 minutes, rotating halfway through baking. Transfer the baking sheets to wire racks. Let the cookies cool completely.

Meanwhile, prepare either the Ooey Marshmallow Goodness (OMG) or Marshmallow Frosting for the filling.

After the cookies have cooled, transfer half of the cookies, flat side up, onto a tray. Using either a scoop or a piping bag with a starred tip, top each cookie with either marshmallow cream or marshmallow frosting.

Add another cookie flat side down to the top to create a cookie sandwich, or creme pie. Refrigerate the pies for 20 minutes to firm up the filling before serving.

Store in an airtight container for up to 5 days.

swoon pies

MAKES 10 PIES

A rounded s'more dipped in chocolate? What's not to love! We loved making these in our cafe and for special events. These "Swoon" pies are great to make ahead and bring to a potluck. You can even swap out the Vanilla Marshmallows (page 18) for Ooey Marshmallow Goodness (OMG) (page 48) and freeze for a twist on an ice cream sandwich. —KAT

Gluten-Free Graham Crackers (page 57)

Vanilla Marshmallows (page 18)

Melting chocolate

Salted-Caramel Sauce (page 54) (optional)

Prepare the graham crackers as directed, but instead of scoring square shapes, use a 3-inch round cookie cutter to cut round circles in the dough. You should end up with about 22 circles, and the remaining dough can be reshaped to fill the cookie cutter or baked in any shape and crushed for Graham Cracker Crust (page 65).

Prepare the Vanilla Marshmallows, but instead of pouring into a pan, scoop the marshmallow mixture into piping bags and pipe a dollop of marshmallow onto half of the graham cracker circles. Top each marshmallow with a bare graham cracker and gently press to combine. Allow to set for at least an hour before dipping.

Prepare the melting chocolate in a large bowl. Using a fork, submerge the sandwich into chocolate until fully covered. Lift up and allow the excess chocolate to drip back into the bowl. Slowly lower onto a piece of parchment until the chocolate is matte and dry.

VARIATION

salted-caramel swoon pies

Add a layer of Salted-Caramel Sauce (page 54) to the base of the first graham cracker. Continue to layer the marshmallow and the other graham. Place in the freezer for 5 minutes, until the salted caramel is firm. Then proceed with the remaining steps of the recipe.

whoopsie pies

What happens when your cake and brownie recipes get stuck together? You end up with a fudgy chocolate masterpiece. We had these available for a limited time at our cafe and the customers would line up for "whoopsie day"! These "whoopsies" are a bit denser than traditional desserts with a similar name, but we think that makes them all the better. —KAT

1 cup semisweet chocolate chips or chopped chocolate

⅓ cup unsalted butter

1 teaspoon instant coffee or espresso powder

2 large eggs, room temperature

¾ cup granulated sugar

¼ cup packed light-brown sugar

1 teaspoon vanilla extract

1¾ cups all-purpose flour, sifted

¼ cup cocoa powder

½ teaspoon baking powder

½ teaspoon kosher salt

1 to 2 tablespoons canola or vegetable oil

Marshmallow Frosting (page 66)

In a medium microwave-safe bowl, combine the chocolate chips and butter. Heat in the microwave on 50 percent power at 30-second intervals until melted, stirring between each interval. Once melted, stir in instant coffee. Pour into the bowl of a stand mixer fitted with a paddle attachment. Allow to cool slightly.

Once cooled, add the eggs one at a time. Then add the sugars and vanilla extract. Beat on medium speed until well combined. The mixture should be lighter and fluffy.

In a separate bowl, sift together the flour, cocoa powder, baking powder, and salt. Add about ¼ cup of the dry ingredients at a time, scraping down the sides of the mixer as needed. Mix on low speed until no more streaks of flour are visible. The mixture will be very thick. Add canola or vegetable oil, 1 tablespoon at a time, to thin the batter.

Cover the bowl with plastic wrap and allow to cool at room temperature for 30 minutes or in the fridge for 20 minutes.

Preheat the oven to 350°F. Line two baking sheets with parchment paper and set aside.

Use a small cookie scoop or a tablespoon to spoon a heaping scoop of dough onto the baking sheet. Set cookies about 2 inches apart. The dough will spread a bit once settled, which is normal.

continued

Bake 8 to 10 minutes until the edges are set and the center is matte and slightly cracked. Remove from the oven.

While still warm, you can reshape any cookies that got a bit misshapen. Simply use the back of a spoon to nudge the edges into a round shape, or use a round cookie cutter to create perfectly uniform rounds. Let sit for 10 minutes before transferring to a wire cooling rack. Allow to cool completely.

Meanwhile, prepare the Marshmallow Frosting. Once the cookies are cool, pipe a layer of marshmallow frosting onto the flat side of half the cookies. Sandwich the cookies by pairing a frosted cookie half with an unfrosted half. Enjoy right away or store in the refrigerator for up to 3 days.

VARIATIONS

chocolate chip cookie pies

Omit the chocolate and coffee and add ¼ cup mini semisweet chocolate chips with the vanilla extract. Once filled, roll the sides of the pies in more mini chips.

peppermint mocha pies

Add 1 teaspoon of peppermint extract to the frosting and roll the edges of the sandwiched cookie in crushed peppermint or candy cane pieces.

strawberry pies

Omit the chocolate and coffee and add ¼ cup powdered strawberry and 2 to 3 drops pink food coloring to the cookie base. Add 1 tablespoon strawberry extract to the frosting.

happy birthday baby-marshmallow cookies

MAKES 24 COOKIES

One of my all-time favorite TV shows is *Gilmore Girls*. I rewatch it at least once a year. There is a hilarious scene in which Rory has spelled "Happy Birthday" on the table with Mallomars for Lorelei to enjoy. When Lorelei sees it, she eats one off the table and then goes to the cabinet, pulls out a box of Mallomars, and replaces the one she's eaten. Of course, this sends Luke into a frenzy. He doesn't understand why she didn't just eat one from the box. She explains she wants to eat one of the ones Rory set up for her but replaces it because she doesn't want the "Happy Birthday" to get messed up. Luke doesn't understand why she didn't just eat one from the box because it's the same process, but, as usual, he just *doesn't get it*. At this point, I've probably seen this episode some fifteen-plus times, and it cracks me up every single time because it is 100 percent something I would do. In honor of those silly Gilmore Girls, we created a birthday cake inspired by Mallomars. Now . . . go spell whatever you want with them. **—LINDZI**

1 cup unsalted butter, softened
⅛ teaspoon kosher salt
½ cup confectioners' sugar, sifted
1¾ cups all-purpose flour, sifted
¼ cup cornstarch
½ teaspoon vanilla extract
¼ cup rainbow nonpareils, plus more for decorating
Vanilla Marshmallows (page 18) or Ooey Marshmallow Goodness (OMG) (page 48), with sprinkles added to batter
Melting chocolate

In the bowl of a stand mixer with a paddle attachment (or using a hand mixer), beat the butter, salt, and sugar on medium speed until creamed, about 5 minutes. Scrape the sides.

Add the flour, cornstarch, vanilla, and rainbow nonpareils to the bowl. Beat on low speed until the dough comes together and there are no white streaks in the dough. *Do not overmix!*

Flip the dough onto plastic wrap. Wrap tightly and refrigerate for at least 30 minutes or up to 2 days.

On a lightly floured surface or between two pieces of parchment paper, roll the dough to ¼-inch thickness and cut into a desired shape. I used a 1¼-inch round cookie cutter. Alternatively, you can roll your dough into a log and cut rounds roughly ¼-inch thick.

continued

Preheat the oven to 350°F. Place the cut shapes on a parchment-lined plate in the freezer for approximately 15 minutes to chill.

Bake on parchment-lined baking sheets for 12 to 16 minutes, rotating tray positions halfway through baking. Shortbread cookies are pale, and you will know they are done when the edges are slightly brown. Cool completely.

Once cool, scoop the freshly made marshmallow or marshmallow cream into a piping bag. Pipe a dollop of marshmallow onto each cookie. Pull straight upward and twist to create a slightly coned shape. Let set (if marshmallows) or chill in fridge for 30 minutes (if using marshmallow cream).

Melt the melting chocolate and dip each cookie into the chocolate. Place on a sheet of parchment paper to cool. Add extra sprinkles to the outside, if using.

Store in an airtight container at room temperature for up to 1 week.

rocky road ice cream
(two ways)

lindzi's way

Growing up, rocky road was my favorite ice cream flavor. I used to pick the marshmallows out of the ice cream and save them for last, eating one little bowl of frozen marshmallows. I should have known then that someday I'd be considered one of the world's leading marshmallow enthusiasts. While Kat's the kind of girl who is looking to make her homemade ice cream from scratch . . . me? I'm looking to eat my ice cream NOW!

1 pint of chocolate ice cream of your choice

1 cup of Ooey Marshmallow Goodness (OMG) (page 48)

½ cup chopped pecans (traditional rocky road uses almonds, but my Texas roots are showing, and I personally prefer to make it with pecans)

This is probably one of the easiest recipes in the book, which is why I love it. Scoop out as much chocolate ice cream into your bowl as you'd like. Add the marshmallow cream and the pecans to the bowl. Mix everything together and enjoy paired with your favorite '90s movie. Catch me eating a bowlful while shamelessly watching *Clueless*.

If you have more time or are just ready to take your ice cream–making skills to the next level, try Kat's version of this recipe.

kat's way

Ice cream is one of my favorite guilty pleasures. I love making my own ice cream at home, so I thought I would include a simple base to make Rocky Road Ice Cream from scratch! The chocolate is so creamy, plus you get to decide how much is enough. Get crazy and add flavored marshmallows, or swap out the almonds for another nut or coconut!

chocolate ice cream base

6 large egg yolks

2 cups heavy cream

1½ cups semisweet chocolate

1½ cups whole milk

⅔ cup granulated sugar

⅛ teaspoon kosher salt

1 teaspoon vanilla extract

1 cup roasted almonds, chopped, store-bought or roasted by hand

2 cups marshmallows, any flavor, roughly chopped

Lightly beat the egg yolks in a small bowl and set aside.

In a heavy-bottom saucepan, heat 1 cup of the heavy cream over medium heat to a simmer. Add the chocolate and whisk continuously until the chocolate is fully melted. Add the remaining cup of heavy cream and stir over low heat until fully mixed. Remove from heat, pour into a medium bowl, and set aside.

In a new medium pot over medium heat, add the milk, sugar, and salt. Whisk until it has warmed and thickened. Then take a ¼ cup of the mixture and slowly stream into the bowl with the egg yolks. Stir continuously but slowly; the goal is to temper the egg yolks and not scramble them.

Next, slowly add the egg yolks to the milk mixture and stir to combine. Let the mixture come to a simmer and thicken. The base is done when it coats the back of a spoon or spatula.

Place a sieve over the chocolate mixture and pour the milk custard base into the chocolate mixture. This will catch any egg yolk bits that have cooked too much. Toss the remnants. Add the vanilla extract to the chocolate base and stir everything together.

continued

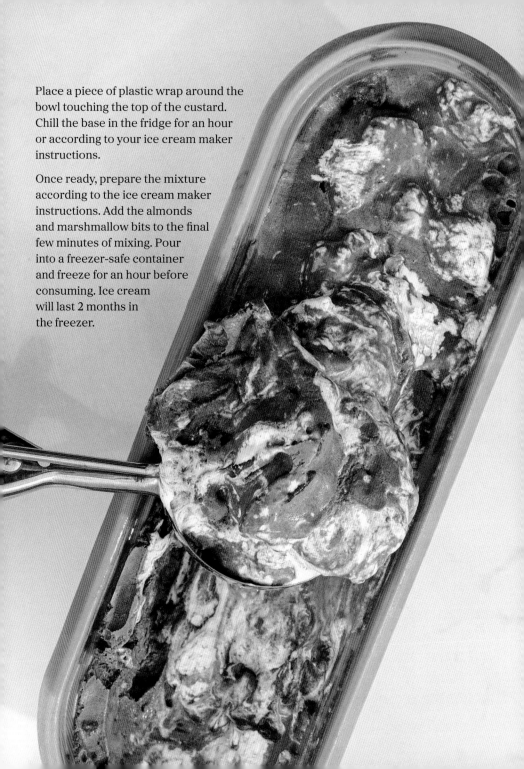

Place a piece of plastic wrap around the bowl touching the top of the custard. Chill the base in the fridge for an hour or according to your ice cream maker instructions.

Once ready, prepare the mixture according to the ice cream maker instructions. Add the almonds and marshmallow bits to the final few minutes of mixing. Pour into a freezer-safe container and freeze for an hour before consuming. Ice cream will last 2 months in the freezer.

pink & white cookies

During the summers, I used to visit my grandparents in New York City, and we would often walk up for a slice of pizza or a cool Italian ice, or go down the street to the corner deli and bakery. There, I would find the biggest, *cutest* black-and-white cookies. You could never find them in Chicago. They were fluffy, almost like a cake, and almost as big as my face. They used to remind me of Cruella de Vil because of their half-white and half-chocolate icing. Immediately, I looked for inspiration from the great Ina Garten and adapted her recipe with browned butter and the addition of almond extract, which gives these cookies a toasted flavor that pairs well with the OMG topping. I knew this recipe just had to be included in our book—with an absolutely XO Marshmallow twist—PINK! **—KAT**

cookies

- **¾ cup unsalted butter**
- **1¾ cups all-purpose flour or gluten-free flour**
- **½ teaspoon baking powder**
- **¼ teaspoon baking soda**
- **½ teaspoon kosher salt**
- **1 cup granulated sugar**
- **1 large egg, room temperature**
- **2 teaspoons almond extract**
- **⅓ cup sour cream**

marshmallow cream

- **Ooey Marshmallow Goodness (OMG) (page 48)**
- **2 to 3 drops of pink food coloring**
- **2 teaspoons lemon juice or 1 teaspoon lemon oil extract (optional)**

continued

Preheat the oven to 350°F. Set aside two baking sheets lined with parchment paper.

In a small saucepan, brown the butter on medium-low heat. The butter will start to bubble in the first 1 to 2 minutes and then will start to darken. Lightly swirl the pan as it continues to heat, but do not stir! The butter is ready when it is dark brown and has a nutty scent, about 5 minutes. Remove from heat and allow to cool slightly. The browned butter will reduce in volume; you need about 5 ounces for this recipe.

In a medium bowl, whisk together the flour, baking powder, baking soda, and salt. Set aside.

In the bowl of a stand mixer fitted with a paddle attachment, cream together the browned butter and sugar on medium speed, until light and fluffy, about 3 minutes.

Once the sugar and butter has creamed, add the egg and almond extract, scraping down the sides after mixing.

Alternate adding in the flour mixture with the sour cream, mixing until just combined and scraping down the sides between each addition.

Using a ¼ cup measuring cup or a cookie scoop, spoon the batter onto the prepared baking sheets. Make sure to leave about 3 inches between each cookie, as they will spread a bit when baking. Bake for about 16 to 18 minutes, until the edges are golden and the center is springy but not wet. Be sure to rotate the pans from front to back about halfway through baking. Allow to cool for a few minutes on the baking sheet before transferring to a wire rack to cool completely.

Prepare the marshmallow cream. Scoop approximately a cup of the cream into a small bowl and add 2 to 3 drops of pink food coloring. Add the lemon juice or lemon extract for additional flavor, if using. Carefully mix until just combined; be careful not to deflate the cream too much.

Once cool, flip the cookies so the flat side is facing upward. Using a spatula or a piping bag, spread half of the cookie with the plain marshmallow cream and half the cookie with the pink marshmallow cream. Let sit out for a few minutes to set.

Pink & White Cookies are best served within 2 to 3 days. To store, lay them on a single layer in an airtight container. Store at room temperature.

5

celebrate with marshmallows

Nearly every memory we have of marshmallows includes other people. Whether it's sipping hot cocoa around the table with friends or toasting up s'mores on a family camping trip, we knew we wanted to include opportunities for people to share their marshmallows and treats with those they loved. So, from birthdays to anniversaries to a random, fun-filled Friday night, you do not necessarily *need* an occasion to celebrate with XO Marshmallow. We are down to party all the time!

s'mores board

I'm known for being a bit of a charcuterie aficionado (if there is such a thing). At any party or function, you can be sure that I'm bringing the perfect selection of meats and cheeses (and other accoutrements) displayed beautifully on a board (see my Instagram if you don't believe me). I've mastered the art of the salami rose and the pepperoni river. My brie cheese has cute cutouts, and my jam selections are always on point. It's the sort of board that's almost too pretty to eat. I started to wonder if I could take that same flair for predinner snacks and add it to the dessert menu with a beautifully laid out s'mores board. After practice (and many a party), I've perfected the ultimate s'mores board. The key? Variety and presentation, presentation, presentation (and homemade marshmallows, of course). The beautiful thing about creating something like a s'mores board is that, ultimately, there's no one answer. It's all about your tastes and what makes your heart (and tummy) happy. Have fun with it; s'mores should never be taken *too* seriously! —LINDZI

3 to 4 marshmallow flavors

2 to 3 types of chocolate

3 to 4 types of cookies/ grahams

Filler candies/fruits

Sterno S'mores Heat fuel can or tabletop firepit (optional)

OUR FAVORITES

MARSHMALLOW FLAVORS: Vanilla, Salted Caramel, Cookies and Cream, Nutella, strawberry, and Funfetti are always crowd-pleasers.

TYPES OF CHOCOLATE: We recommend variety—have milk-, dark-, and white-chocolate options. I also like to have caramel sauce at the ready or a caramel-filled chocolate. Reese's Peanut Butter Cups are great for peanut butter lovers, or Kit Kats for an extra crunch.

TYPES OF COOKIES/GRAHAMS: Our Gluten-Free Graham Crackers (page 57), chocolate chip cookies, donuts (cut in half horizontally, down the middle), and Oreo cookies all make for excellent s'mores "bases."

continued

FILLER CANDIES/FRUITS: We love adding fruit to s'mores! Apples, strawberry slices, and banana slices all add a freshness to your s'more. Have some sour options too! Sour Patch Kids, Airheads, and peach rings not only look beautiful on your board but add the perfect pucker to your s'more.

If you're using a Sterno or a firepit, I like to start by putting it in the center of the board. It allows you to build a focal point for your board and to build everything else around it.

If you're not using a Sterno and will be roasting your s'mores over a fire instead, that's totally fine! We want to start with the biggest (and most important things) first–the marshmallows! Take a few of each marshmallow flavor and group them together in different sections of the board. The key is to not be too symmetrical with how you lay things out.

The number of marshmallows you'll need depends on the size of the board. You'll want the marshmallows to take up about one-third of your board.

Next, add the grahams/cookies around the marshmallows. I like to fan one out, take one and weave it through like a river, and stack another to help create more dimension. See the diagram for more details.

Next, add the chocolate in a similar manner to the cookies. I like to put the chocolates next to the mallow flavors that I think they would pair well with (i.e., Funfetti next to white chocolate). It just makes it easier on your guests to help show them what goes best together.

Finally, take your "filler" pieces of fruits and extra candies and fill in any blank spaces on the board. This allows your board to look very full and highly stylized.

lindzi's top s'mores board tips

1. Think about the time of day you'll be serving your board. If first thing in the morning, consider adding fresh fruit to go with a mimosa. Later in the day? Maybe opt for a bit of sparkle to make your board really stand out.
2. Limit your color palette. Trust us. When you're actually shopping for items to include on your board, sticking to two to three color options will help you make decisions. Plus, it will keep your board looking chic and cohesive.
3. Don't be afraid to mix and match! Pairing different textures and flavors keeps your board visually interesting and fun to eat. I like to think of the main groups as: crunchy, soft, sweet, and sour. A mix of cookies, marshmallows, chocolate, and sour candies ought to do it!

campfire cookies

I have to let you in on a little secret. My husband, Drew, makes the world's BEST chocolate chip cookies. I may be a marshmallow maven, but this man knows his chocolate chip cookies. Lucky for us, he was kind enough to let me share that recipe with you for us to make the cutest and most delicious campfire cookies ever. Or, if you just want to make the cookies all by themselves, I totally get it. —LINDZI

chocolate chip cookie base

- ½ cup butter, melted
- ½ cup sugar
- ½ cup packed dark-brown sugar
- 1 teaspoon vanilla extract
- 1 large egg
- 1⅓ cup gluten-free flour
- ½ teaspoon baking soda
- ½ teaspoon coarse salt
- ½ cup semisweet chocolate chips

garnish

- 1 (5-ounce) bag gummy bears
- 1 (8-ounce) bag pretzel sticks
- 20 Vanilla Marshmallows (page 18)
- 40 log-shaped chocolate chewy candies
- 1 (16-ounce) container green frosting, or Marshmallow Frosting (page 66) with 3 drops green food coloring

To make the cookies, brown the butter in a small saucepan over low heat. Pour the butter into a medium mixing bowl and let cool for 1 minute.

Add both sugars to the bowl and mix with a spatula until smooth. Then add the vanilla and egg, mixing until combined. Add the flour, baking soda, and salt. Continue to mix until combined.

Fold in the chocolate chips to the mixture. Cover and cool in the refrigerator for at least 30 minutes.

Using spoons or a small cookie scoop, scoop out 20 scoops of cookie dough and place onto baking sheet. These should be about 2 inches apart.

Bake the cookies at 350°F for about 12 minutes. If you want wider, crispier cookies, remove them from the oven after 6 minutes and drop/slam the cookie sheet onto the baking rack from a couple inches above. This helps the cookies spread out more. Then return the sheet to the oven to finish baking.

Add a sprinkle of kosher salt to the top of the cookies once they are removed from the oven. Let the cookies cool on a baking sheet.

continued

Once the cookies are cool, add green frosting to the top of them and smooth out the frosting in circular motions with a spoon.

Pull out the orange, red, and yellow gummy bears from the bag. Cut them up into smaller pieces (I know, I hate this part too!!) and put them in the middle of the cookies so they look like a campfire. Snack on the other colors of gummy bears while you work.

Take 4 pretzel sticks and put them around the bears in a point so they look like wood on a campfire.

Cut the marshmallow squares into fourths and put one on top of each pretzel stick. Roast them for more of a campfire effect. I typically wait to roast them until right before serving.

Add 2 chewy chocolate candy logs to the outside of the "campfire." These are meant to look like logs you would sit on around the campfire. Serve and enjoy!

omg-filled cupcakes

MAKES 12 STANDARD-SIZE CUPCAKES

As much as we love chocolate cake, sometimes you need a smaller snack—like our marshmallow cream–filled cupcakes. This recipe is a bit denser, more chocolaty (and we think better) than most cupcake recipes. It also holds up well with the marshmallow cream and optional Marshmallow Frosting. OMG-Filled Cupcakes can be toasted before being served and easily colored and flavored to suit your next event. **—KAT**

Unflavored nonstick pan spray

1 tablespoon instant coffee or instant espresso

½ cup boiling water

1 cup all-purpose flour

1 cup granulated sugar

¼ cup cocoa powder

½ teaspoon baking soda

½ teaspoon baking powder

½ teaspoon kosher salt

2 large eggs, room temperature

½ cup sour cream, room temperature

4 tablespoons vegetable oil

1 teaspoon vanilla extract

1 cup Ooey Marshmallow Goodness (OMG) (page 48), for filling (and topping, optional)

1 batch Marshmallow Frosting (page 66), for frosting (optional)

Prepare a 12-cup cupcake pan by spraying with unflavored nonstick pan spray. Set aside.

In a small bowl, whisk together the coffee and hot water. Set aside.

Preheat the oven to 350°F.

In a medium bowl, whisk together all the dry ingredients until well combined. This can be done by hand or in the bowl of a stand mixer.

Add the eggs, sour cream, vegetable oil, and vanilla to the mixture, stirring thoroughly between each addition. Slowly stream in the coffee and mix until the batter is uniform and has thinned out. Pour into the prepared cupcake pan, filling about two-thirds of the way.

Bake for 25 to 30 minutes, until a toothpick inserted into the center comes out clean. Remove from oven and let cool completely.

Once cool, use either a knife or the end of a spare pastry decorating tip to create a hole in the center of each cupcake that goes about halfway to the center.

Fill a piping bag with the marshmallow cream and fill the hole of each cupcake with the cream. You can then either use the remaining marshmallow cream to frost the cupcakes or whip up a batch of Marshmallow Frosting to finish the job!

Frosted cupcakes should be stored in an airtight container in the fridge for up to 5 days or at room temperature for up to 3 days. Unfrosted cupcakes can be baked and frozen for up to 1 month.

walking s'mores

I'm quite well-known for the phrase "if you aren't getting messy eating a s'more, you aren't doing it right!" However, sometimes you really do want a s'more without all of the mess. Cue the Walking S'more. It's exactly what it sounds like . . . a s'more you can take on the go, getting all the gooey goodness of a s'more without having to worry about getting your hands messy. —LINDZI

12 bags Teddy Grahams, or substitute with Annie's Gluten Free Bunny Grahams placed inside small plastic bags

2 cups chocolate chips, or 4 chocolate bars

24 Vanilla Marshmallows (page 18)

There are two easy ways to make a walking s'more!

option 1
(my personal favorite!)

Open your Teddy Graham bags and sprinkle in chocolate chips or squares of chocolate bars to your desired level of chocolate. Toast a Vanilla Marshmallow over a campfire (or stovetop) until it's nice and gooey. Put the marshmallow in the bag (make sure it's not on fire!) and use the outside of the bag to spread the gooey marshmallow around until everything inside is melted and extra messy. Stick your fork in and thank me!

12 bags Teddy Grahams, or substitute with Annie's Gluten Free Bunny Grahams placed inside small plastic bags

6 cups chocolate pudding (optional)

2 cups chocolate chips, or 4 chocolate bars

24 Vanilla Marshmallows (page 18)

option 2
(great if you are on the go and do not have access to a fire)

Open your Teddy Graham bags and temporarily dump out the bears. Add half a cup of chocolate pudding to the bottom of the bag. Add the bears back to the bag. Top with chocolate chips or squares of chocolate. Take your Vanilla Marshmallows and cut them into fourths with a knife or kitchen scissors. Sprinkle those into the bag and mix it all together using a spoon. Enjoy!

s'mores cake

Did you know that the term "s'mores" was coined by the Girl Scouts in the 1920s? I wanted to create a cake honoring the traditional campfire treat, which involved many hours of playing with flavors and ideas until we agreed this was the one!

The S'mores Cake may look like it has a lot of elements, but it's actually quite simple to assemble. If you've attempted to make Gluten-Free Graham Crackers (page 57), Chocolate Ganache (page 52), or our Marshmallow Frosting (page 66), you're already halfway through making this cake. Grab your spatula and meet me at the campfire. —KAT

for the spiced vanilla cake layers

Unflavored nonstick pan spray

1 cup all-purpose flour

1 cup granulated sugar

1 teaspoon baking powder

¼ teaspoon kosher salt

1 teaspoon ground cinnamon

¼ teaspoon ground nutmeg

¼ cup unsalted butter, melted

¼ cup vegetable oil

1 egg, room temperature

½ cup buttermilk, room temperature

2 teaspoons vanilla extract

for the chocolate cake layers

Unflavored nonstick pan spray

1 cup granulated sugar

¾ cup all-purpose flour

½ cup unsweetened cocoa powder

1 teaspoon baking soda

½ teaspoon baking powder

½ teaspoon kosher salt

¼ cup semisweet chocolate, chopped

½ cup hot brewed coffee

1 large egg

6 tablespoons sour cream

¼ cup vegetable oil

2 tablespoons water

2 tablespoons vanilla extract

for the lapsang souchong ganache filling and frosting

1 cup heavy cream

2 heaping teaspoons lapsang souchong tea

9 ounces semisweet chocolate chips

½ teaspoon vanilla extract

Marshmallow Frosting (page 66)

¼ cup Gluten-Free Graham Cracker crumbs (page 57), plus more for decorating

continued

spiced vanilla cake layers

Preheat the oven to 350°F. Spray two 6-inch pans with unflavored nonstick pan spray and set aside. **NOTE:** For even easier prep, line the pans with parchment paper and a bit of pan spray.

In a large bowl, whisk together the flour, sugar, baking powder, salt, cinnamon, and nutmeg.

Add the melted butter, oil, and egg to the dry ingredients. Whisk until just combined. There should be no flour visible.

Then add the buttermilk and vanilla extract and whisk until combined. Use a spatula to scrape down the sides of the bowl and ensure an even mix.

Transfer half the batter into each prepared pan, about 10 ounces per pan.

Bake for 30 to 34 minutes, or until a toothpick inserted in the middle returns with a few crumbs.

Remove the pans from the oven and allow to cool completely before transferring the cakes to a cooling rack. This cake can be made in advance and, once cool, wrapped tightly in plastic wrap and frozen for a month. Allow to cool to room temperature before frosting.

chocolate cake layers

Preheat the oven to 350°F. Spray two 6-inch pans with unflavored nonstick pan spray and set aside. **NOTE:** For even easier prep, line the pans with parchment paper and a bit of pan spray.

In a medium bowl, whisk together the sugar, flour, cocoa powder, baking soda, baking powder, and salt. Set aside.

In a large bowl, add the chocolate and pour the hot brewed coffee on top. Allow to sit for 3 to 4 minutes, then whisk until the chocolate is smooth and all the chips are melted.

In the large bowl with the chocolate, whisk in the egg, sour cream, oil, water, and vanilla extract until combined.

Add the flour mixture to the large bowl in two parts, scraping down the sides of the bowl after each addition. Mix until smooth.

Transfer half the batter into each prepared pan, about 12 ounces per pan.

Bake for about 25 to 30 minutes, or until a toothpick inserted in the middle returns with a few crumbs.

Remove the pans from the oven and allow to cool completely before transferring the cakes to a cooling rack. This cake can be made in advance and, once cool, can be wrapped tightly in plastic wrap and frozen for a month. Allow to come to room temperature before frosting.

lapsang souchong ganache

In a small saucepan, heat the heavy cream on medium-low heat until just simmering. Then remove from heat and add the lapsang souchong tea. Allow to sit on the counter and steep for about 20 minutes.

Strain the tea from the heavy cream and return the infused cream to a small saucepan. Heat on medium heat until the heavy cream just starts to climb up the side of the pan, about 2 to 3 minutes. Remove from the heat.

In a medium bowl, add the chocolate chips. Then pour the cream over the chocolate chips and allow to sit for 5 minutes. Using a whisk, stir the mixture until the chocolate is smooth and glossy. Add the vanilla. Allow to rest on the counter until thick and cooled, about 30 minutes.

The ganache will hold for about a month in the fridge if kept in an airtight container.

to assemble

Trim the tops of each cake layer so they are flat and approximately the same height. Do not worry if you have a few imperfections; frosting fixes everything!

On a cake plate, smear a small amount of marshmallow frosting and place a layer of spiced vanilla cake.

Using a piping bag, pipe a border of Marshmallow Frosting extending about an inch and a half toward the center. Add a dollop of Marshmallow Frosting to the center of the cake, creating a "bull's-eye." Then spoon in a layer of chocolate ganache to the ring space left without frosting. Sprinkle 2 tablespoons of crushed grahams on top of the ganache and frosting. Carefully top with a layer of chocolate cake and repeat the filling process. Top that layer with a layer of vanilla cake and repeat the filling process. Top that layer with the last layer of chocolate cake, placing it "top down" so that the top of the cake has an even layer to frost.

At this point, your frosting may have started to soften. If needed, place the cake in the fridge for 20 to 30 minutes until the frosting has "chilled," and this will give you an easier surface to coat.

Frost the cake with marshmallow frosting, adding additional frosting between the layers if needed. Again, if the frosting starts to soften, simply pop the cake back in the fridge for about 20 minutes to firm up.

Before serving, top with toasted marshmallows, broken graham crackers, and pieces of chocolate. You can also add a chocolate drip with some leftover chocolate ganache, and sprinkle with crushed graham cracker crumbs. Have fun!

continued

NOTES: You can bake these cakes together if you have four 6-inch pans! About halfway through baking, rotate the pans from front to back. Note that one cake flavor may be ready before the other.

Cracked cake? One cake turned out a bit heavier than the other? No problem. Stick your cracked cake layer in the middle and use some extra frosting as "glue." Plop your heavy cake as the base layer so it can support the weight of the rest of the cake. No one needs to know!

dessert fondue:
when i dip, you dip, we dip!

We are both pretty much obsessed with the '60s and '70s. The style, the fashion (just check our closets), and, of course, the fondue! But you don't have to throw a '60s-themed party to enjoy a delicious dessert fondue. Fondue is great for any gathering—holiday parties, summer nights on a patio, or any reason to gather with friends and family. Who doesn't love to dip things in chocolate? Are we right or are we right? Everyone brings cake or cookies . . . so why not dip those (and marshmallows!) into chocolate?! After all, when I dip, you dip, we dip! With the rise of the popularity of dessert boards, fondue takes them to the next level by creating dessert board fixings that you dip into chocolate (or caramel, if that's your thing!). Lindzi's favorite part is that it looks incredibly labor intensive and fancy but really does not take much effort to achieve a beautiful (and yummy) fondue.

Chances are if you have the items to make a cake in your house, you have the ingredients to make fondue. The main thing we want to focus on is presentation. Whether you're like Lindzi and refuse to use anything except a vintage '70s bright-yellow fondue pot that belonged to her husband's grandmother, or if you have a new one from the store, all you need are some amazing "dippables" and people to share them with to create a fabulous fondue experience. —KAT AND LINDZI

½ cup heavy cream

8 to 10 ounces chopped semisweet or bittersweet chocolate

3 tablespoons Grand Marnier or other, similar liqueur

Bonus: Add in chopped white chocolate for a swirl

In a saucepan, gently heat the cream over low heat until steaming. Remove from heat and stir in the chocolate until melted.

Add the liqueur to the chocolate mixture. The liqueur is what helps keep the chocolate smooth and melted.

Transfer the chocolate to a fondue pot.

Keep over a very low flame such as a tea light candle or Sterno to avoid burning the chocolate. Stir every now and then.

continued

DIPPABLES SUGGESTIONS

- Marshmallows, of course! We recommend the classics: vanilla, Nutella, cookies and cream, and salted caramel.

- Graham crackers.

- Fruits: We recommend strawberries, raspberries, blackberries, and apple slices.

- Cookies: Shortbread cookies, Oreos, and fan cookies are great.

- Donuts: You read that right! We love a good cruller donut for chocolate dipping.

Once you have your chocolate and dippables ready, you know what to do . . . Dip and enjoy! If you're looking for a way to elevate the display of your dippables, check out our S'mores Board recipe (page 117).

sweet potato pie

MAKES ONE 9-INCH PIE

Thanksgiving is one of my favorite holidays. Why? It's a day filled with sharing meals with friends and family—what could be sweeter? In my house, we make "candied yams," a mix of canned yams, cinnamon, maple syrup, and marshmallows. The whole thing is layered up and thrown into the oven, emerging as our sweetest side dish. I decided to adapt our favorite family tradition into a pie.

I used our Graham Cracker Crust (page 65) for a dense, crunchy layer. Then, combining roasted sweet potatoes, fall spices, and a splash of bourbon, we've got a smooth and luxurious filling. Of course, you need the toasted marshmallow cream for the final touch. Your family will be fighting over every slice, guaranteed! —KAT

Graham Cracker Crust
  (page 65)
2 medium sweet potatoes,
  roasted and peeled
1 tablespoon maple syrup
6 tablespoons butter,
  softened
¼ cup heavy cream
2 tablespoons bourbon
  whiskey

⅔ cup packed dark-brown
  sugar
1 large egg, 2 large egg
  yolks
1 teaspoon vanilla extract
1 teaspoon ground
  cinnamon, plus extra for
  dusting
¼ teaspoon ground
  nutmeg

¼ teaspoon ground
  allspice
¼ teaspoon ground
  cardamom
¼ teaspoon kosher salt
Ooey Marshmallow
  Goodness (OMG)
  (page 48)

FOR THE CRUST: Make the Graham Cracker Crust recipe and press into a 9-inch pie pan.

TO PREPARE THE FILLING: Preheat the oven to 425°F. Poke a couple of holes into each sweet potato and roast in the oven until soft, about 45 minutes. Remove from the oven and allow to cool slightly. Decrease the heat to 350°F.

Remove the peels from the sweet potatoes and cut into large chunks. Add to the bowl of a stand mixer fitted with a whisk attachment. Mix until the sweet potatoes are thoroughly pureed.

Add the maple syrup, butter, and heavy cream to the bowl. Mix on medium speed until smooth. Add the whiskey and dark-brown sugar to the mixer and whisk until combined. With the mixer on low speed, add the egg yolks and spices. Mix until combined.

Add the filling to the pie crust and bake in the oven for 50 to 60 minutes. The pie is finished when the center is no longer jiggly. Remove from the oven and allow to cool.

Using a spatula, top the pie with the marshmallow cream. Top with a dash of the cinnamon, if using. When ready to serve, use a culinary torch to toast the marshmallow cream.

salted-caramel marshmallow popcorn balls

MAKES 12 LARGE OR 20 SMALL POPCORN BALLS

I feel like you either grew up making popcorn balls or you just didn't. I am the latter. I associate popcorn balls with either commercially made, break-your-teeth Halloween treats or little old grandmas who are making them for Christmas and later will be making sweaters for all the grandkids to open on Christmas Day. Either way, they just missed my radar, and for this I must apologize to all my fellow popcorn lovers out there because these are SO DANG GOOD!

Marshmallow popcorn balls are like a crunchy, salty snack meeting a crispy treat. Here, the Salted-Caramel Marshmallows (page 33) enhance the caramel notes of the brown sugar and give them a bit of a softer, ooey, gooey texture. Making them was super easy and pretty quick! I loved the look of adding a little Rolo candy to the top of my popcorn balls so that they look like little ornaments. —KAT

12 cups popped popcorn, or ²/₃ cup kernels

½ cup salted butter

½ cup packed light-brown sugar

¼ cup corn syrup or honey

¼ teaspoon salt

1 teaspoon vanilla extract

4 cups Salted-Caramel Marshmallows (page 33) (about 16 marshmallows)

12 to 20 Rolo candies, to top popcorn balls

Fun sprinkles, chocolate chips, or food coloring (optional)

Place a sheet of parchment paper on a large baking sheet. Set aside.

Place the popped popcorn in a large bowl. Set aside.

In a large 3-quart pot, add the butter, sugar, corn syrup, and salt. Cook over medium heat, stirring constantly until the mixture comes to a boil. Turn the heat to low and continue cooking for about 4 minutes, swirling the pot occasionally.

Remove from the heat. Add the vanilla and the Salted-Caramel Marshmallows. Stir until all the marshmallows are melted—be careful because the mixture will be extremely hot! If using, add a couple of drops of food coloring into your mix.

continued

Pour the marshmallow mixture over the popcorn and, using a wooden spoon, stir until all the popcorn is coated. Then mix in your desired add-ins (sprinkles, chocolate chips, etc.).

As soon as the mix can be handled, form popcorn into balls and set on the prepared baking sheet. Use any remaining marshmallow mixture from the bowl as "glue" for attaching the Rolo candies to the tops of the completed popcorn balls. Repeat until all the popcorn mixture is used.

Let the popcorn balls rest at room temperature until cool, about an hour. Then move them into an airtight container or into individual treat bags.

You could easily swap in another flavor of marshmallow. Kahlúa Marshmallows (page 29) would work well for a holiday cocktail party, or Vanilla Marshmallows (page 18) with a crushed chocolate sandwich cookies could represent "lumps of coal" for your naughty family members.

Once finished and wrapped in treat bags, gift the popcorn balls to friends and teachers, or place them around the table for the holidays.

Popcorn balls are best consumed within 48 hours but can last a few days if kept in an airtight container. After that, they will get a bit soft/chewy.

Happy popping!

hot cocoa bar

As a Texas transplant who found herself smack-dab in the middle of the Midwest (and Midwest winters), I was not prepared for how seriously Midwesterners took their hot cocoa. We were a packet-with-water-in-a-microwave kind of family. It's no wonder hot cocoa was never a go-to treat for me. I would just eat all the marshmallows off the top (and keep adding more and more) and ignore the rest of the cup. When I told Kat how we made cocoa growing up, I swear I saw a tear run down her face! She gasped and explained that, in her house, chocolate was beautifully made on the stove using milk. Once we created XO, we figured there had to be a lovely middle ground—something that was easy but also rich and decadent. Our Gourmet Hot Cocoa Mix was born, and from that, we began to create beautiful hot cocoa bars and stations for events. Our "Hey, Hot Stuff, Hot Cocoa Bar" will show you how to create an adorable hot cocoa station at home that will make your guests fall in love with every cup—and it's easy enough to replicate for even just a fun winter weekend treat! —LINDZI

Perfect Cup of Hot Cocoa recipe (page 74)

Milk or nondairy beverage of your choice

2 to 3 flavors of marshmallows

Whipped cream

Peppermint sticks or candy canes

Roller wafer cookies

Chocolate chips

Any other "toppings" of your choice

A boozy extra like Kahlúa or Irish crème (optional)

Cute signage

Fun mix of mugs

Let's get that display going! I like to set everything up first and give each topping its own container. You can go for a matchy-matchy look and make all of the containers the same, or you can use different styles for each topping. I like to use various vintage containers I've found over the years at thrift and antique stores. It adds extra character and style to your cocoa bar. It also helps add various heights and dimensions to your bar, which only serves to make it look more elevated.

Arrange all your containers in order of how people will make them. If you're making your own hot cocoa, have it in a large ready-to-serve container at either the beginning of your bar (if you want people to form a line) or in the center if you're looking for a more stylized look. If you're using a mix, have those containers and cups at the beginning of the bar with your milk and nondairy beverages next in line.

continued

When arranging the toppings, we like to put the marshmallows in the most prominent containers because they are the largest and will take up the most space on top of the cup. Don't forget to include little tongs or spoons for your guests to use to add their various toppings. Once your cocoa is all made, enjoy!

1. Pick a theme. Are you doing a Christmas hot cocoa bar? A winter hygge theme? A boozy hot cocoa brunch? Something extra colorful and fun for the kids? Having a fun, set theme will help you figure out the best marshmallow flavors, toppings, and even serveware for your hot cocoa bar.

2. Mix and match. I've mentioned it before, but it bears repeating—mix and match your serveware. Find some fun vintage dishes and mugs from your local thrift store or antique shop. It adds more depth and texture to your cocoa bar. Plus, you can find different serveware for different themes without spending much.

3. Be playful. It's a hot cocoa bar—it's supposed to be FUN! Don't overthink it. Play with different toppings you may not normally think of, like gummies or rock candy. The best hot cocoa bars are the ones that make even grown adults feel like kids again!

gingerbread house: marshmallow style

MAKES 1 RIDICULOUSLY FUN GINGERBREAD HOUSE

One of my favorite holiday memories is building a gingerbread house with my younger sisters. We were known to get a little wild and crazy with our decor choices (there was a Hello Kitty gingerbread house creation that is still discussed only in hushed tones). We never stuck to the design on the box. We bought extra materials to be able to do things like change the roof structure and even create extra people for the house. One of the extra ingredients that was always on the must-have list were mini marshmallows. They come in handy for so many things, like corner joints or for building little people for your house.

After we started XO, I realized we could even use marshmallow cream as an alternative to frosting, and it blew my mind because not only did it hold better but it tasted so much better too! After all, the best part of building a gingerbread house is destroying it and eating it later, right? Just me? **—LINDZI**

1 gingerbread house kit of your choosing (you can be fancy and make your own, but I like to keep it easy)

1 to 2 piping bags of Ooey Marshmallow Goodness (OMG) (page 48)

1 Vanilla MarsHalo™ for a wreath (page 21)

1 piping bag of green frosting

1 piping bag of pink frosting

Different types of candy and sprinkles

Marshmallow Snowmen (page 144)

Follow the instructions on your kit for how to begin to assemble your gingerbread house

Instead of the kit's icing, use the piping bag of marshmallow cream to connect the house pieces together. This will hold stronger, bond faster, and taste more delicious.

Use the piping bag of marshmallow cream to create snow and icicle details on the house/roof.

Take the MarsHalo™ (donut-shaped marshmallow) and use the green frosting and dab small drops on it to make it look like a wreath.

Use the pink frosting to draw a bow on top of the wreath.

Use the marshmallow cream to attach the wreath to the roof.

Use all of your other candy and sprinkles to decorate and make the cutest house ever.

Head to the Marshmallow Snowmen recipe (page 144) to create some cute marshmallow people to live in your gingerbread house.

marshmallow snowmen

MAKES 12 SNOWMEN

Would you believe me if I told you I've never made a snowman before? Growing up in Texas, we didn't have a lot of snowfall, and certainly not enough to create a full person made of snow! I was always jealous of the kids who got to experience a full winter. Maybe that's part of the reason why I moved to Chicago.

Now that I'm older and have seen my fair share of Chicago snow, I found that I personally prefer to enjoy my winter from the comfort of my own house instead of the outdoors, which is why I created these adorable marshmallow snowmen, who take up their residence at the top of my hot cocoa. Delicious and warm—just like I prefer my winter days. **—LINDZI**

36 Vanilla Marshmallows (page 18)

1 bag pretzel sticks

1 black food-grade marker

1 orange food-grade marker

1 package red gel frosting or pull-apart red licorice

Make your Vanilla Marshmallows.

Connect three Vanilla Marshmallows together using pretzel sticks until you have three marshmallows stacked on top of each other.

Add two pretzel sticks to the side of the middle marshmallow as "arms" and two pretzel sticks to the end of the bottom marshmallow as "legs."

Draw three circles in a vertical line on the middle marshmallow to create "buttons."

Draw three circles on the top marshmallow for "eyes," and draw additional circles to create a "mouth."

Use the red gel frosting (or red licorice) to create a scarf at the base of the top marshmallow. Plop into a cup of hot cocoa and enjoy!

s'mores kit

I am one of those people who is obsessed with gift giving. I will make up a holiday just to be able to create something for you. Dog's dentist appointment? I've got you. National "you're so cute, so have a gift" day? I'm there. One of my go-to gifts is a s'mores kit. While you can choose a great number of combinations for this kit, I personally love to pair our Salted-Caramel Marshmallows (page 33), Ghirardelli's caramel-stuffed chocolate squares, and our Chocolate Graham Crackers (page 62) for a salty, sweet, ooey, gooey dream. That said, there are so many other great s'mores kit combos out there, and I really can't wait to see what you come up with! **—LINDZI**

24 marshmallows (flavor of your choosing)

Enough chocolate for 24 s'mores (depends on the chocolate you are using and how it is divided; personally, I really love using Ghirardelli's individual squares because you can get them in so many different flavors)

48 homemade graham crackers (choose the flavor based on your s'more)

The hardest part of putting together a cute s'mores kit is finding the right vessel to hold everything. I put all the above ingredients (divided by four) into a clear sealable bag to keep them fresh longer. I stack them as follows: eight graham crackers, four squares of chocolate, and four marshmallows—all wrapped into a bag.

Now the next step is to make it cute! Choose your vessel depending on your occasion. You can add a bow to your clear bag. Put the bag in a fabric bag or a reusable wooden box—anything that works for your gift. One of my favorite ways I ever gave these as gifts were in pink purses that included reusable skewers and a Sterno—they gave such glamping vibes.

marshmallow cocktails

Most people think only of hot cocoa when it comes to adding marshmallows to a beverage. A few have even unlocked the magic of adding marshmallows to their morning coffee instead of cream and sugar. I tell anyone who will listen to add our Lavender-Honey Marshmallows (page 22) to their Earl Grey tea to create an instant London Fog (page 25). If you haven't tried one, drop what you are doing right now and go make one (you're welcome).

So many people are missing out on one of my favorite ways to level up your favorite cocktail: with marshmallows! From the perfect S'more-tini to a Marshmallow Old Fashioned, hostesses with the mostess-es know that marshmallows make for a delicious cocktail. So, cheers, chin-chin, *salut,* and more to three of my favorite marshmallow cocktails. **—LINDZI**

espresso s'mortini

MAKES 1 COCKTAIL

1 tablespoon melted chocolate

1 tablespoon crushed Gluten-Free Graham Crackers (page 57)

1 ounce coffee liqueur

1 ounce Kahlúa

½ ounce marshmallow vodka

Ice

1 skewer

1 to 3 marshmallows, for garnish

To rim the glass, melt your chocolate and dip the rim of your glass in it. While still wet, dip the chocolate rim into crushed graham crackers. Set aside.

In a cocktail shaker, combine the coffee liqueur, Kahlúa, and marshmallow vodka with ice. Shake until mixed well.

Strain the mixture into your rimmed cocktail class. Skewer your marshmallow(s) and toast them to your preference. Lay the skewer across the top of your glass and serve.

marshmallow phony negroni mocktail

MAKES 1 MOCKTAIL

1¼ ounce zero-alcohol gin (we prefer Ritual)

1¼ ounce zero-alcohol aperitif (again, we prefer Ritual or Lyre's)

1 to 2 Orange Marshmallows (page 44), for garnish

1 large ice cube

Stir all of the drink ingredients together and pour over the large ice cube in a rocks glass. Top the drink with the desired marshmallow amount—I prefer mine on a skewer.

marshmallow old fashioned

- **2 ounces of your favorite bourbon (we recommend one with smoky notes)**
- **½ tablespoon simple syrup**
- **½ teaspoon bitters**
- **½ teaspoon chocolate bitters**
- **1 large ice cube**
- **1 to 3 marshmallows, for garnish (Honey Marshmallows are the best, page 30)**

Stir all of the drink ingredients together and pour over the large ice cube in a rocks glass. Top the drink with the desired number of marshmallows. Toast the marshmallows more than you normally would. The extra char really adds to the campfire taste. I add mine straight to the drink so that they melt right into the liquid. You can also add them on a skewer if you prefer more of a garnish.

metric conversions and equivalents

volume

¼ teaspoon	1 milliliter
½ teaspoon	2.5 milliliters
¾ teaspoon	4 milliliters
1 teaspoon	5 milliliters
1¼ teaspoons	6 milliliters
1½ teaspoons	7.5 milliliters
1¾ teaspoons	8.5 milliliters
2 teaspoons	10 milliliters
1 tablespoon (½ fluid ounce)	15 milliliters
2 tablespoons (1 fluid ounce)	30 milliliters
¼ cup	60 milliliters
⅓ cup	80 milliliters
½ cup (4 fluid ounces)	120 milliliters
⅔ cup	160 milliliters
¾ cup	180 milliliters
1 cup (8 fluid ounces)	240 milliliters
1¼ cups	300 milliliters
1½ cups (12 fluid ounces)	360 milliliters
1⅔ cups	400 milliliters
2 cups (1 pint)	460 milliliters
3 cups	700 milliliters
4 cups (1 quart)	.95 liter
1 quart plus ¼ cup	1 liter
4 quarts (1 gallon)	3.8 liters

weight

¼ ounce	7 grams
½ ounce	14 grams
¾ ounce	21 grams
1 ounce	28 grams
1¼ ounces	35 grams
1½ ounces	42.5 grams
1⅔ ounces	45 grams
2 ounces	57 grams
3 ounces	85 grams
4 ounces (¼ pound)	113 grams
5 ounces	142 grams
6 ounces	170 grams
7 ounces	198 grams
8 ounces (½ pound)	227 grams
16 ounces (1 pound)	454 grams
35.25 ounces (2.2 pounds)	1 kilogram

length

⅛ inch	3 millimeters
¼ inch	6 millimeters
½ inch	1¼ centimeters
1 inch	2½ centimeters
2 inches	5 centimeters
2½ inches	6 centimeters
4 inches	10 centimeters
5 inches	13 centimeters
6 inches	15¼ centimeters
12 inches (1 foot)	30 centimeters

to convert	multiply
Ounces to grams	Ounces by 28.35
Pounds to kilograms	Pounds by .454
Teaspoons to milliliters	Teaspoons by 4.93
Tablespoons to milliliters	Tablespoons by 14.79
Fluid ounces to milliliters	Fluid ounces by 29.57
Cups to milliliters	Cups by 236.59
Cups to liters	Cups by .236
Pints to liters	Pints by .473
Quarts to liters	Quarts by .946
Gallons to liters	Gallons by 3.785
Inches to centimeters	Inches by 2.54

To convert Fahrenheit to Celsius, subtract 32 from Fahrenheit, multiply the result by 5, then divide by 9.

description	fahrenheit	celsius	british gas mark
Very cool	200°	95°	0
Very cool	225°	110°	¼
Very cool	250°	120°	½
Cool	275°	135°	1
Cool	300°	150°	2
Warm	325°	165°	3
Moderate	350°	175°	4
Moderately hot	375°	190°	5
Fairly hot	400°	200°	6
Hot	425°	220°	7
Very hot	450°	230°	8
Very hot	475°	245°	9

1 cup uncooked white rice = 185 grams
1 cup all-purpose flour = 125 grams
1 stick butter (4 ounces • ½ cup • 8 tablespoons) = 115 grams
1 cup butter (8 ounces • 2 sticks • 16 tablespoons) = 225 grams
1 cup brown sugar, firmly packed = 220 grams
1 cup granulated sugar = 200 grams

Information compiled from a variety of sources, including *Recipes into Type* by Joan Whitman and Dolores Simon (Newton, MA: Biscuit Books, 1993); *The New Food Lover's Companion* by Sharon Tyler Herbst (Hauppauge, NY: Barron's, 2013); and *Rosemary Brown's Big Kitchen Instruction Book* (Kansas City, MO: Andrews McMeel, 1998).

Andrews McMeel Publishing
a division of Andrews McMeel Universal
1130 Walnut Street, Kansas City, Missouri 64106

www.andrewsmcmeel.com

25 26 27 28 29 SDB 10 9 8 7 6 5 4 3 2 1

ISBN: 978-1-5248-9517-4

Library of Congress Control Number: 2024952744

Editor: Jean Z. Lucas
Art Director: Holly Swayne
Production Editor: Elizabeth A. Garcia
Production Manager: Chadd Keim
Photographer: Lauren Sims Photography
Food stylist: Isabel Gonzalez Creative

attention: schools and businesses

Andrews McMeel books are available at quantity discounts with bulk purchase
for educational, business, or sales promotional use. For information, please email the
Andrews McMeel Publishing Special Sales Department: sales@andrewsmcmeel.com.